G. J. BOLUS.

106   £1

D1341735

LIVING IT UP
Or,
They Still Love Me in Altoona!

LIVING IT UP

or

They Still Love Me in Altoona!

by

GEORGE BURNS

W. H. ALLEN · LONDON
A Howard & Wyndham Company
1977

First British edition, 1977

Printed in Great Britain by Fletcher & Son Ltd, Norwich
for the Publishers, W. H. Allen & Co. Ltd,
44 Hill Street, London W1X 8LB
Bound by Richard Clay (The Chaucer Press) Ltd, Bungay, Suffolk

ISBN 0 491 01828 2

Acknowledgment and thanks are made by George Burns and G. P. Putnam's Sons to Jerry Vogel Music Co.,
Inc., 121 West 45th Street, New York, N.Y. 10036 for permission to reproduce the chorus of "I'll Buy the
Ring" and "Change Your Name to Mine." Words by Ed. Rose and Wm. Raskin, Music by Jack Mills, Copy-
right © 1919; Copyright Renewed and Assigned by Rose Raskin to Jerry Vogel Music Co., Inc./To Warner
Brothers, Inc. for "The Red Rose Rag" (Percy Wenrich-Edward Madden) © 1911 Warner Bros., Inc., Copyright
Renewed, All Rights Reserved, Used by Permission./To United Artists Music Publishing Group, Inc. for permission to publish the following lyrics from "When Francis Dances With Me" by Ben Ryan and Violinsky Leo
Feist, Inc. Printing of the following lyrics, "She does a new step it goes one, two three, kick. She can't count so
good that's the worst of the trick. My shin bones look like they've been hit with a brick when Francis dances
with me." © 1921, Renewed 1948 Leo Feist, Inc., New York, N.Y.

Contents

A special thanks to Elon Packard and Jack Langdon, who were a great help to me in writing this book.

LIVING IT UP
Or,
They Still Love Me in Altoona!

A Day in the Life of
a Late-Blooming Author!

Getting to be my age didn't happen overnight. I'm eighty years old, and I had a damned good time getting there. I run into a lot of people who ask me when I'm going to retire. I think the only reason you should retire is if you can find something you enjoy doing more than what you're doing now. I happen to be in love with show business, and I can't think of anything I'd enjoy more than that. So I guess I've been retired all my life.

In the first place, I don't see what age has to do with retirement. I've known some young men of eighty-five, and I've met some very old men of forty. In a sense that's what this book is all about; getting old doesn't mean that you have to stop having fun. When you're twenty-one you can enjoy yourself by going out with a twenty-one-year-old girl, and when you're eighty you can enjoy yourself by going out with an eighteen-year-old girl.

I got news for you. There isn't a thing I can't do now that I didn't do when I was twenty-one . . . which gives you an idea of how pathetic I was when I was twenty-one. (That's a lie, but I might as well tell you something right here at the beginning of the book. Anytime I can get a laugh I'm not going to let the truth interfere with it.)

Look, there's nothing wrong with going out with young girls. I enjoy meeting young girls. I figure some of their youth may rub off on me, and some of what I've got might rub off on them—that is, if it doesn't drop off before I meet them.

11

But I mean it—young girls are stimulating. They get you out of the house, and when you get older that's important. If you've got a date, it gives you an incentive. You shower . . . you shave . . . you choose your best cologne . . . you pick out your best shirt . . . your best tie . . . your best suit . . . and try to look as good as you can possibly look for your age. And it works. The other evening I had a date, and after I got dressed I stood in front of the mirror and I looked so good I said to myself, "Maybe that eighteen-year-old girl is too old for me!" (I'm sorry, there I go again.)

Now, I have a close friend, George Pallay, who's a seventy-five-year-old bachelor, and really a case. He's generous, he's charming, he's good company, fun to be with, but he's got one hangup. Whenever he's out with a young girl he gets embarrassed and introduces her as his niece. He's good for three or four nieces a week.

Actually he isn't fooling anybody. One night he walked into a restaurant with a young girl and said to the captain, "Could my niece and I have that corner table in the bar?"

The captain said, "I'm sorry, Mr. Pallay, but another one of your nieces is sitting there with George Burns."

That upset Pallay. He liked my niece better than the one he had with him.

Just the other day I tried to reason with him. We were having coffee after a leisurely lunch, and I said to him, "Pallay, everybody knows that these girls are not your nieces. Who do you think you're kidding? Why do you go to all that trouble? You take them to nice places, you enjoy each other's company, why don't you just relax and forget about this silly niece business?"

He looked at me sheepishly and said, "I'm embarrassed about what people might think."

"What do you care what people think?" I said. "You like the girl, the girl likes you, you've had a wonderful evening, and that's what life is all about."

He paused, let it sink in, and then said, "George, you're absolutely right. I'm going out with a young girl tonight and

I'm not going to introduce her as my niece. I'll just have her tell people I'm her uncle."

I said, "Pallay, I'm glad you got the message."

However, I don't want you to get the impression that this book is only about young girls. Oh, they're bound to crop up here and there—about every page or so—but they're not the important part of the book.

What's important when you get to be my age is to enjoy what you're doing. Now the young people today have a saying: "Do your own thing." Well, I go along with that, but I'd like to add something to it: "Do your own thing, but make sure you're happy doing it!"

Even when I'm doing nothing I find a happy reason for not doing it. That's the way I've been all my life. No matter what I did, I was happy doing it at that time. Back when I was a small-time vaudeville actor and couldn't get any jobs, I was still happy because I was out of work in a business that I loved.

I remember when I was sixteen I worked for Mersky & Co. in New York. They manufactured middy blouses, and I was a cutter. At that time Mersky was having a problem because nobody was buying his middy blouses, so I came up with a brilliant idea.

I said to him, "Mr. Mersky, I know how you can unload all these middy blouses. Send every store in town thirteen dozen with an invoice which says, 'Enclosed find twelve dozen middy blouses.' Even though they didn't order them, they'll keep them because they'll figure they're getting thirteen dozen for the price of twelve."

Mersky said, "Do you think it'll work?"

I said, "Mr. Mersky, trust me, it can't miss."

A big smile broke out over Mersky's face, and he gave me a $2 raise right on the spot—which brought my salary up to $16 a week.

Two weeks later he called me into his office. I got all excited—I could see the sign out front reading MERSKY AND BURNS. But as soon as I walked into his office and saw the

13

expression on Mersky's face, I knew our partnership just dissolved.

He said, "Burns, remember that idea you came up with a couple of weeks ago about the middy blouses?"

I said, "Yes, sir, did it work?"

"Certainly it worked—but not for me, for them it worked! Everybody I sent thirteen dozen middy blouses to kept the extra dozen and sent back twelve!"

Already showing my talent as a straight man, I said, "Really?"

Mersky said, "But, Burns, I'm a man of my word. I gave you a two-dollar raise, you still got it. But only until six o'clock tonight—then you're fired!"

Even this made me happy. Again I could go back to vaudeville and be out of work in a business that I loved.

But eighty is a beautiful age. It takes very little to turn me on. And sometimes when I think I'm turned on I find out I'm not even plugged in. What's the use of kidding—I've reached the point now where I can get by on about one half inch of happiness. A whole inch would overstimulate me! But who cares, I'm enjoying it.

This is what I'm trying to say. The secret of feeling young is to make every day count for something. To me there's no such thing as taking a day off. When I'm not working, which isn't often, my day goes something like this:

I usually get up at eight o'clock—sometimes earlier, but never later. I like getting up early, it gives me a longer day and more time to do things. Okay, now I'm up. The first thing I do is go to the bathroom, and in the bathroom I do what everybody does—brush my teeth. All right, so that's the second thing I do—the first thing I do is gargle. Look, I've got to take care of my vocal cords.

Now I'm wide awake and ready for my back exercises. They're not strenuous, and I have fun doing them. First, I lie on my back on the floor and grab my left knee with both hands and pull it up as far as I can, trying to touch my chin. I do this ten times with each leg. Then, still on my back, I

14

rotate my legs in the air as though riding a bicycle. I do this twenty-five times. Now I sit on the edge of the bed and bend over and touch the floor with my hands, first to the left and then to the right. I do this twenty times.

And that's it! I feel that these particular exercises are good for me. I've always had a bad back, but I don't worry about it. If I outlive my back, fine—if my back outlives me, I'll stop doing my exercises.

Anyway, now it's time for breakfast. Those exercises always make me feel good, and when I feel good I sing. So on my way downstairs I usually sing a chorus of "Honeysuckle Rose." Breakfast consists of a piece of fresh fruit in season or a glass of orange juice, some coffee, and cornflakes. I love cornflakes. When I chew them they make a noise in my mouth . . . and when I hear that noise I think it's applause . . . and when I hear applause I go into the second chorus of "Honeysuckle Rose."

Naturally, while I'm having breakfast I read the morning papers. I think everybody should read newspapers because I feel that one should ebulliently endeavor to be cognizant of the necessity for amelioration of global détente! (Look, I didn't write that last line, I copied it out of *Time* magazine. I thought the book could use a little class.)

And then of course, I read the theatrical trade papers, the *Daily Variety* and the *Hollywood Reporter*. The first thing I look at is the obituary column. If my name isn't in it, I sing another chorus of "Honeysuckle Rose."

All right, now I'm ready for my walk. But walking can be awfully dull if you do nothing but just walk. So enjoy the beauty around you. Look at the birds! Look at the flowers! Look at the trees! And if a pretty girl passes, look at her legs! If you're worried about cheating on your wife, look at only one leg!

I do my walking in the garden; ten minutes every morning at a pretty fast clip. And while I'm walking, I rehearse. I run through the lyrics to my songs and go over the jokes in my monologues. My gardener loves my monologues because I do them out loud, but he always laughs in the wrong places. It isn't that my monologues aren't funny, it's just that he doesn't speak English. If I could learn to do my jokes in Japanese, I'd have him rolling in the rosebushes.

By now it's 9:30 and time to get upstairs and into the bathroom again—I love to gargle. After a good gargle I shave and then into the shower. While I'm in the shower I sing "In the Heart of a Cherry." I'd sing "Honeysuckle Rose," but by now I'm sick of it.

Picking out my wardrobe for the day is something I enjoy, because clothes have always been important to me. I came from a very poor family, and all my clothes were handed down to me by my older brother. When he outgrew a suit he gave it to me, and when I outgrew it I gave it to my younger brother. When my older brother had it, it was a blue suit; when I got it it was green; and by the time it reached my younger brother it was a sort of washed-out purple.

I was sixteen before I owned a suit of my own. I don't know how I managed to get the $12 to buy it, but I was really proud of that suit. I thought I had finally made the big time. It was a gray plaid suit and it had a four-button coat. I would only button the top button so that I could fold back the bottom part of the coat and put my hand in my pants pocket. I thought this gave me a jaunty look, and people would think I had money in my pocket. Believe me, the only thing I ever had in that pocket was my hand. I kept my hand in that pocket so long that when I outgrew the suit and gave it to my younger brother, my hand was still in the pocket.

But things have changed since then. Now I have a much larger wardrobe. I've got a closetful of suits, but mostly I wear sports clothes; jackets, slacks, and turtleneck sweaters. I think everybody should try to look as good as he possibly can. I knew an actor, Jack Desmond, seventy-two years old. He wore a wavy toupee, had his nose straightened, his face lifted, and his teeth capped. He looked gorgeous. He

16

looked so good nobody knew he was dead. In fact, his wife still thinks she's cheating on him.

Now, where was I? Oh, yes, I'm dressed for the day and ready to leave for the office. If I'm staying home that night I stop off in the kitchen to tell my cook, Arlette, what I want for dinner. Arlette has been working for me for years, and when I walk into the kitchen, she says, "Mr. Burns, you look beautiful this morning!" That's why she's been with me for years.

Driving to General Service Studio where I've had my office for twenty-three years is another experience. While I'm driving along I smile at people in the other cars because I think everybody knows me. But everybody doesn't. Those who know me smile back, and those who don't know me think I'm an idiot. But I say if you're going to be an idiot, you might as well smile and let people think you're enjoying it.

At ten sharp I walk into my office, and my secretary, Jack Langdon, says, "Mr. Burns, you look beautiful this morning!" He's been with me for years, too.

I go into my inner office, and my writer, Elon Packard, says, "Hiya, George!"

He's only been with me ten years and he's a good writer, but he still doesn't know what to say in the morning.

We work in the office from ten until noon. As I said earlier, this is my schedule when I'm not actually working. It's only two hours but it's very concentrated effort. We answer correspondence, update the routines in my stage act, write speeches for testimonial dinners, plan what I'm going to say on the talk shows, write copy for various commercials I do . . . it's really a full two hours.

But at twelve o'clock on the nose, I quit. We could be in the middle of writing a comedy routine, and sometimes Packy follows me all the way out to my car, hollering, "George, wait a minute, I've got a great finish for the routine!" But I don't hear him. At twelve o'clock I turn my

17

head off. Anyway, I get in my car, check in the rearview mirror to see if my smile is working, and I'm off to Hillcrest Country Club.

Hillcrest Country Club is like a second home to me. It's a beautiful club and located very conveniently in Beverly Hills only ten minutes from my home. I've belonged to Hillcrest for over forty years.

Now, they have a large membership, and I know practically all of them—but not by name. I remember faces, but when it comes to names I've got a very bad memory. So I've got a little system that works for me—I call everybody Kid. When I come into the club and somebody says, "Hello, George," I answer, "Hello, Kid."

I remember one afternoon coming into the club with Jack Benny, and as we headed for the dining room one of the members came up to us and said, "Hello, George."

I said, "Hiya, Kid," and started to go on.

But the guy stopped me and said, "Wait a minute, George, you and I have been members of this club for years, and you always call me Kid. You don't even know my name."

I looked at him and said, "I don't, huh." Then, turning to Jack, I said, "Jack, tell him his name," and kept walking.

Jack turned to the man and quickly said, "I'll see you later, Kid," and hurried after me.

Of course, it's a little different when I run into Adolph Zukor, who's one hundred and two years old. A man that age deserves respect. When he says "Hello, George," I say, "Hello, MISTER Kid."

But Adolph Zukor is a remarkable man. I remember when he had his hundred and second birthday. After Mr. Zukor had his lunch, the waiter brought in this big cake to surprise him, and all the members sang "Happy Birthday." So I went over to him and said, "Mr. Zukor—" (This time I remembered his name because it was written on the cake.) —I said, "Mr. Zukor, how does it feel to be one hundred and two years old?"

He said, "George, I feel just as good now as I did two years ago."

At Hillcrest when I have my lunch I always sit at the same table. It's called the "Round Table." The reason it's called the Round Table is because it's a table that's round. (I hope I made that clear. My publisher told me to keep nothing from you.)

Anyway, this table is where the action is. There's very little listening but an awful lot of talking, because most of the people who sit there are in show business. Every day the cast changes—you might find Groucho Marx, Danny Thomas, Georgie Jessel, Milton Berle, and directors and producers like Eddie Buzzell, Pandro Berman, George Seaton, etc. With that bunch if you want to get a word in edgewise, you have to have an appointment. The conversations cover everything. You can hear opinions on politics, sports, religion, music—you name it, and we're all experts on it.

But over the years I've noticed a change at the table. Where the main topic used to be our sex lives, it's now about our bad backs. I can't speak for anybody else, but I know how I got my bad back—taking bows.

As in every group there is usually one person who takes charge. At our table it's Georgie Jessel. He knows all the jokes, he's a great storyteller, and he's very funny. But he does one thing that drives me up the wall. Whenever he's scheduled to do a eulogy at someone's funeral, he tries it out on us. Did you ever try eating lunch and listening to a eulogy at the same time? Jessel is the only one I know who can turn matzos, eggs, and onions into the Last Supper.

Since I'm on the subject, I'd like to tell you one story. Years ago in New York there were two great actors named Sam Bernard and Louie Mann. Jessel was crazy about Sam Bernard, they were very good friends, but he just didn't like Louie Mann. Well, Sam Bernard died, and Jessel did the eulogy at the funeral. He was absolutely marvelous; it affected everybody . . . he cried . . . we cried . . . Jessel was in top form.

Anyway, a couple of weeks later I happened to meet Jessel walking down Broadway, and he was wearing a black coat, a black tie, and striped pants. Right away I knew he was on his way to do another eulogy, so I said, "Georgie, who died?"

He said, "Louie Mann, and I'm on the way to do the eulogy."

"But you always told me you didn't like Louie Mann," I said. "How can you do a eulogy for a man you didn't like?"

He replied, "I couldn't pass it up, I've got some great stuff left over from Sam Bernard."

Back to the Round Table.

Groucho Marx has a very fast, caustic wit. He's well informed and extremely humorous—and above all he's loaded with CHUTZPAH! If the right situation comes up, he doesn't mind repeating the same joke twenty times in one day.

Let me give you an example. Years ago Sophie Tucker used to sing a song called "If You Can't See Mama Every Night, You Can't See Mama at All." Now I've been sitting at the Round Table for forty years, and every time I order sea bass, without fail Groucho will say, "If you can't sea bass every night, you can't see Mama at all." I laughed the first time I heard it, but after hearing it for forty years it sort of loses its freshness.

One day I wanted to order sea bass for lunch, but Groucho was sitting at the table and I didn't want to hear that lousy joke again. So I took the waiter aside and I quietly whispered, "I'll have some sea bass."

And the waiter quietly whispered back, "If you can't sea bass every night, you can't see Mama at all."

After hearing that line again from the waiter I decided it was time to change my diet. I went back to the table and said, "Groucho, do you have any jokes about whitefish?"

He said, "No, George."

I turned to the waiter and said, "I'll have some whitefish."

And Groucho said, "If you can't see whitefish every night, you can't see Mama at all."

I told you he had chutzpah!

Lunch usually takes about an hour or so, and then I'm off to the card room for my favorite recreation—playing bridge. I love the game; it's exciting, stimulating, and it makes you think. I don't say I'm the greatest bridge player in the world but the men I play with are just as bad as I am. I could say they're worse than I am, but that doesn't sound modest. . . . I'll say it anyway; they are worse than I am.

Sometimes I've watched some of the great bridge players play, and it's always so very quiet. They concentrate, they take their time, they speak softly—you can hear a pin drop. The table I play at sounds like a bowling alley on Saturday night. Nobody concentrates, everybody's in a hurry, and we're all screaming at the same time. That's the kind of bridge that relaxes me.

We argue, we fight, and the language we use didn't come out of *Rebecca of Sunnybrook Farm*. But there's a reason why we carry on like this—all the men that I play bridge with are practically my age or even older; sometimes I'm the youngest at the table. So we holler and shout to make sure the other members of the club know that we're still living. The only time we get quiet is when Georgie Jessel comes over to kibitz. It makes us very nervous because we know he's got four eulogies in his pocket.

One day a new member, a very distinguished attorney, came over and asked to join our game, and he did. He was lucky enough to draw me for a partner. The very first hand our opponents bid opened with a spade and their finishing bid was three no-trump. I doubled, which called for a spade lead, but my partner, this brilliant attorney, led the three of diamonds. I was shocked. I slowly folded my cards and laid them gently on the table, placed my cigar carefully in the ashtray, took three deep breaths to get some oxygen into my head, and then said to him, "Look, you may be one of our great attorneys . . . you're very well dressed . . . you're a fine looking man . . . you're over six feet tall . . . which makes you one of the tallest idiots I've ever played with!"

He looked straight at me, then stood up and said, "I'm sorry, gentlemen, I've had enough. And, Mr. Burns, I would just as soon you would never talk to me again. I've never been called an idiot in my life."

"If I stopped talking to you, I'd have to stop talking to everybody at this table, because we're all idiots," I answered.

He thought this over for a moment, then he sat down, smiled, and said, "Mr. Burns, the tall idiot is back in the game." From then on he was a member of our group, screaming and hollering like the rest of us.

I don't recommend our way of playing bridge to everybody. There are times when it could lead to violence. But if you do play it our way, you better have a sense of humor. I remember a few years ago I was playing bridge at the Beverly Hills Bridge Club with George Raft, Harpo Marx, and Mack Gordon, who was one of our most prolific songwriters. He wrote "Time on My Hands," "Chattanooga Choo-Choo," "Did You Ever See a Dream Walking?"—I could go on and on.

Anyway, Mack Gordon was a very stubborn bridge player who wanted to play every hand. But I knew his game because I had played with him before. Well, in this particular rubber he was my partner, and he bid a spade. I had a heart bust—eight hearts to a queen—and no spades. In other words, I had nothing. So I bid four hearts. Now in bridge this meant I was telling my partner that this hand could only be played in hearts and for him to pass. But not Mack Gordon.

As I said, when he got a bid in his teeth he wouldn't let go. When it came around to him he didn't even look at me, he just laid his cards face down on the table, folded his arms, looked out the window and defiantly hollered, "Four spades!"

When it got to me, I never looked at him. I laid my cards face down on the table, folded my arms, and said, "I didn't

22

know we were playing with somebody across the street, but if we are, I'd like them to hear my bid, too." Then I hollered out the window, "Five hearts!"

Mack stared straight at me, and in a steely, low tone he said, "George, I've got more money than you have—seven spades."

I looked right back at him, and slowly and emphatically said, "No you haven't—seven no-trump!"

Mack threw his cards into the center of the table, stood up, and said, "Let's go downstairs and straighten this out!"

"You mean you want to fight me?" I said.

"That's right," Mack answered.

"All right," I said, "let's go down."

So Harpo, Georgie Raft, Mack, and myself started out. About halfway down the stairs I said to Harpo loud enough for Mack to hear, "I think the greatest song ever written was 'Did You Ever See a Dream Walking?'"

Mack said, "Let's go up and finish the game."

I often wondered what would have happened if I hadn't thought of that line. Mack weighed 300 pounds and I weighed 135. The world might have lost one of its great singers.

Anyway, back to Hillcrest. It's now about four o'clock and it's time for me to go home and take a nap. Oh, by the way, the Hillcrest Country Club also has a beautiful golf course. I quit playing golf several years ago. I found out I wasn't getting any exercise from it. All us members took carts, and the caddies carried our clubs. So the caddies got all the exercise and they looked great; we rode in the carts and looked pathetic.

The truth is I gave up golf because I knew I'd never be good at it. I tried very hard, but I just couldn't put it all together. Lloyd Mangrum, one of our great professional golfers, used to play at our club a lot, and one day in the locker room he said to me, "George, you look perfect . . . that beautiful knitted shirt, an alpaca sweater, those expensive slacks, argyle socks, bench-made golf shoes

23

. . . you've got an alligator bag, the finest matched irons, and the best woods money can buy. It's a damned shame you have to spoil it all by playing golf."

Now, where was I? Oh, yeah, I'm writing a book.

My nap takes about an hour and a half. I usually go to sleep at four thirty and get up at six. I really think everybody should take a nap in the afternoon. I know that when I get up after my nap I'm very refreshed and ready for the evening.

Did you ever notice how easy it is to fall asleep when you take a nap? You just lie down, and boom! you fall asleep in broad daylight. But going to sleep at night is a different story. We make such a big deal out of it. We take a sleeping pill, we put on our pajamas, we scrub our teeth, we set the alarm clock, check the window to see that just enough fresh air is coming in, get into bed and turn out the light, snuggle up under the blankets, close our eyes—and boom! we're wide awake. Then we try lying on our left side, our right side, on our back, on our stomach, and nothing happens. We've made such a production out of going to sleep that we think we're in the sleeping business and we ought to get paid for it.

Now I suppose you're saying to yourself, "Sure, he's told us why we can't sleep, but if he's so clever, why doesn't he tell us how we can get to sleep?"

Well, I'm not one of those writers who leaves you hanging there. All you've got to do is buy my next book, which covers that question. Thank you. I may not be remembered as one of the great writers, but I am polite . . . You'll notice I used three periods—I'm also a generous writer.

Now comes the most relaxing and comfortable time of my day. It's a quiet time and gives me a chance to reflect about life and things in general. Daniel and Arlette are busy in the kitchen preparing dinner, and while I'm making myself a double martini on the rocks my two cats, Ramona and Princess, are purring and rubbing against my legs as though they're anticipating the evening as much as I am.

Of course, I only have these quiet and relaxing evenings when I don't have a date—which means I'm quiet and relaxed about once a month. There I go again, I broke a beautiful mood just to get in one tired joke.

Anyway, when I do have a date, I usually take her to dinner at a nice restaurant. As I mentioned before, I like the company of young girls, and young girls seem to like to go out with me. It's because I don't rush them—there's no pressure on them. When I take them to Chasen's for dinner, in between courses they have time to do their homework.

On occasion if I'm in a romantic mood, I invite the young lady back to my place. And at the end of the evening she won't be disappointed. We have a little brandy, I turn the lights down low, and when I think the moment is just right—I send for my piano player. I sing her four or five songs and go upstairs and go to bed. My piano player takes her home. I've outlived four of my piano players.

Well, that's the end of my day, and it's also the end of the chapter. Being an old vaudevillian, I can't get out of a chapter without a finish—and being a singer, this is my finish. While you're reading it, hum along. I guarantee you'll be whistling it for the rest of your life:

> I'd love to call you Rose, dear,
> But roses fade away,
> Roses die when wintertime appears.
> I'd love to call you Daisy
> But daisies always tell
> What sweethearts love to whisper in your ear.
> I'd love to call you Honey
> But honey runs away,
> I'd much prefer a name like Clinging Vine.
> And if I called you Buttercup,
> The dandelions would eat you up—
> So I'll buy a ring and change your name to mine.

Catchy melody, isn't it?

Writing Humor Is Nothing To Laugh At!

This is the second chapter, and it has absolutely nothing to do with the book. But then again neither did the first chapter. I hope my style of writing isn't as confusing to you as it is to me. However, I remember something that Gracie used to do which might be of great help to you. When she read a book, first she'd read the beginning, and then she'd read the finish. Then she'd start in the middle and read toward whichever end she liked best.

Give that last line a little thought. It may sound like I'm making a joke, and I hope I am.

Well, now on with the chapter. All through my life in show business I've been a very fortunate man. When I first started out in vaudeville and it looked as if I were about to hit bottom, I always managed to bounce back. I didn't bounce very high, so even after I bounced I was pretty close to the bottom.

In those days the acts I did were pathetic, but I loved every minute of it. If I teamed up with a fellow and our act was so bad we couldn't get a job, we'd split up and I was back on the bottom again. But I didn't stay there long. A week later I'd team up with another fellow and come right back with another act that was just as bad. I must have done dozens of bad acts—singing, dancing, rollerskating, dramatic sketches. I even worked with a dog and then a seal. You name it and I've done it. But the important thing is I was in action; I was in show business and I was moving. When you did acts like I did you had to keep moving.

I'll tell you about one act I did when I was eight years old. I know you're not going to believe it, because it's hard for me to believe, but it's a true story and it did happen to me.

I was then singing with the Peewee Quartet. We were all about the same age, and I was the tenor. We used to sing in saloons and pass the hat around. Sometimes we'd make as much as fifteen cents, and to us that was big money. Anyway, we were singing in this saloon on Houston Street on the Lower East Side in New York, and we had just finished our second song, "Mary Ann, Mary Ann, Mary Sat in a Corner," when this man came over to me and said, "Kid, I like the way you sing, how would you like to be in my act?"

I looked up at him and there was this fellow wearing a black coat with a beaver collar, a derby hat, a diamond stickpin in his tie, and a gold chain across his vest with an elks's tooth hanging from it. I was very impressed.

"Yes, sir," I said.

It turned out his name was Jack Frye, and his act was called Jack Frye & Co. He offered me $10 a week.

Well, I had never heard of that kind of money. My whole family put together didn't make that much. I raced home to tell my mother that I got a job for $10 a week.

She listened to me and then said, "But what about your school?"

"But, Mama," I said, "it's ten dollars a week."

"Your education comes first," she said, shaking her head.

"Mama—ten dollars!!!"

My mother paused, giving that a little thought, and then said, "All right, so you'll get smart a week later."

Anyway, after five days of rehearsal Jack Frye & Co. opened at Huber's Museum on 14th Street. Now Huber's Museum was sort of a penny arcade with about ten side-show attractions like the Fat Lady, the Snake Charmer, the Sword Swallower, the Fire Eater, etc. And it also had a little theater where we played. You could come into Huber's Museum and see all of these side-show attractions plus the vaudeville show for fifteen cents.

28

Now, I'm not going to say that this sketch I was in was the worst sketch in the world, because it wasn't that good. The idea of the plot was that Jack Frye had an office—nobody knew what he did there because he didn't want to clutter up the plot with a lot of details. I was a shoeshine boy, and as I was shining his shoes he offered me a job as an office boy. All through the rest of the sketch he tried to test my honesty. And that's the plot.

Here's the way it worked. When the curtain went up, Jack Frye was sitting at his desk looking very dignified and reading *The Police Gazette*. And offstage you heard my voice singing this song:

> Shine, shine, five cents a shine;
> My name is Teddy,
> And I'm always ready;
> My brushes are new,
> My blacking is fine—
> Step right up, five cents a shine.

Then I'd stick my head through the door and say, "Shine, boss?"

Frye's opening line was memorable. He looked at me, put *The Police Gazette* down, and said, "Okay, boy, give me a shine."

As I was shining his shoes he offered me this job, which I took. Then he explained that there was $500 in the desk drawer and that I should protect it with my life, and he exited.

I turned to the audience and said, "I'm so happy that I got this job that I think I'll sing a song." Now wouldn't you think that Frye would have me sing a happy song? Nope—he picked out a sad ballad and told me to cry while I was doing it. There I was, supposed to be so happy about my new job, and I was standing up there crying my heart out.

This was the song:

29

Always think of Mother
No matter where you go.
Always think of Mother
Because she loves you so.
Your friends and many others
Will sometimes prove untrue,
But always think of Mother
'Cause she always thinks of you.

After that heartrending song the plot began to thicken. Frye returned three different times disguised as various characters. First he was a Jewish peddler, then he was an Italian immigrant, and the last one was a tough gangster. Each time he tried to trick me into giving him the $500 from the desk, but I wouldn't budge, I was a loyal office boy. When he finally came in as the gangster and I wouldn't give him the money, he advanced toward me shaking his fist, and angrily said, "Give me that money or I'll break every bone in your body!"

But that didn't frighten me. I knew there was a gun in the drawer, so I opened the drawer and put my hand on the gun, and then I made my big, dramatic speech. It went on for about three minutes and ended up with, "Threaten me if you will, sir, my mother always taught me that honesty is the best policy. Here under this ragged coat deep in my heart these words shall remain there until the last minute of my life!" Then I paused and continued, "Do you still want that money?"

"You better hand it over," snarled Frye.

"All right," I said, "then take that!" And I pulled the gun out of the drawer and pointed it at him.

With that he pulled off his wig and hollered, "Don't shoot, I'm your boss!" Then he put his arm around my shoulder and walked me to the center of the stage, and said, "My boy, your mother is right. Honesty has triumphed once again."

And the curtain came down with a thud!

Well, Jack Frye & Co. lasted one performance, and I was back on the bottom again. But as usual I bounced back. The next day I was singing tenor again with the Peewee Quartet.

My entire career has been filled with ups and downs like that. And if you think about it, I'll bet your life has been the same way. Everybody has his highs and lows. I remember a few years back when there was a quiet couple of months for me and nothing seemed to be happening. I still came to my office at General Service Studios every morning and met with my writer, Elon Packard, and my secretary, Jack Langdon, but this lull made these two kids nervous. They worried that I was nervous, too, so they manufactured things for us to do in order to make me believe we were busy. When I'd walk into the office, Packy would say, "George, I know what we can do today. Let's start out by writing a very funny letter to Jack Benny."

Then Jack Langdon would pipe up with, "Marvelous. And if we finish it in time, we'll send a funny telegram to Carol Channing."

This went on day after day with these two clowns trying to dream up two hours of nothing to make me think I was busy. I went along with it, but I never could figure out why they got so panicky. I was paying them every week; I was calm, but they were nervous wrecks.

One Tuesday morning we were hard at work writing a hilarious note to leave in the bottle for my milkman when the phone rang. Sure enough it was my agent. He told me that the Teacher's Scotch people were putting on a big, nationwide advertising campaign in all the leading magazines and newspapers. These ads featured humorous articles written by various personalities in show business such as Groucho Marx, Redd Foxx, Tommy Smothers, and others. The conversation ended with my agent saying, "George, the Teacher's Scotch people would like you to do one of these. Do you think you'll have time?"

31

I glanced at the other two and said, "Sure, as soon as I finish this note to my milkman I'll get right on it."

Well, there I was, up there bouncing again. I turned to the boys and said, "Fellows, you can now relax, and we'll start on this first thing tomorrow morning. Jack, you put a new ribbon in the typewriter, I'm going to the club, and Packy, you go to your favorite bar and do a little research on Teacher's Scotch." He's very good at researching scotch.

When we met at the office in the morning there was a note from my agent telling me the advertising agency handling Teacher's had suggested this title for the article I was supposed to write: "When Jack Benny has a party, you not only bring your own scotch, you bring your own rocks." They wanted me to let them know what I thought of that title. So I called them up and told them I loved it. Personally, I thought it was much too long, but after all I had a deal with the Teacher's people, and you don't get paid for writing notes to your milkman.

We talked it over in the room, and I decided that since they mentioned Jack in the title they must want an article about Jack Benny and Teacher's Scotch. So this is what I wrote:

WHEN JACK BENNY HAS A PARTY, YOU NOT ONLY BRING YOUR OWN SCOTCH, YOU BRING YOUR OWN ROCKS

By George Burns

That line about bringing your own scotch and rocks is true. But that doesn't mean that Jack Benny is a cheapskate. Don't forget, he furnishes the coasters, the water, the electricity, and the furniture you sit on. To me, that's the mark of a generous man.

Anyway, when they asked me to write this article for Teacher's Scotch they— Hold it!

To show you how generous Benny really is, one time three of us were in a bar having a drink. There was Edgar Bergen,

32

Jack Benny, and myself. We were all drinking scotch. (And being men of good taste, naturally we ordered Teacher's.) When we finished, Jack said, "I'll take the check." So the bartender gave him the check, and he paid it. On the way out, I said, "Jack, it was very nice of you to ask for that check."

Jack said, "I didn't ask for it, and that's the last time I'll have a drink with a ventriloquist."

(But don't forget, you can still sit on Jack's furniture for free.)

Now . . . when they asked me to write this article for Teacher's Scotch they— Hold it! I just thought of another Benny story.

Whenever Jack tries to get clever it always backfires on him. One night the two of us were having dinner at Chasen's restaurant, and he said to me, "George, I've got an idea that's absolutely brilliant. Let's both have the most expensive dinner on the menu, and we'll make Dave Chasen pay for it."

I said, "How are you going to do that?"

"Simple," Jack said, "when the check comes, you and I will get into an argument, I'll call Dave Chasen over, and I'll say, 'Dave, if George Burns pays this check, I'll never come into this restaurant again.' And then you say, 'Dave, if Jack Benny pays this check, I'll never come into this restaurant again.' We're both very good customers, so Dave will say, 'Boys, don't argue,' and he'll tear up the check. Brilliant?"

I said, "Jack, it's a great idea, and it can't miss."

So after dinner we started to argue, and Jack called Chasen over and said, "Dave, if George Burns pays this check, I'll never come into this restaurant again!" I just sat there looking at Jack and never said a word. So Dave gave Jack the check.

Jack said, "George, aren't you going to say something?"

I said, "Sure, Jack, thanks for dinner."

(Now he won't even let me sit on his furniture.)

Well, when they asked me to write this article for Teacher's Scotch they— Hold it.

I just thought of another one. During all the years of my friendship with Jack Benny, whenever we'd talk on the tele-

33

phone I'd always hang up in the middle of the conversation. The first time I did it fifty-five years ago he thought it was very funny. I still do it, but he doesn't laugh at it anymore. The reason I keep doing it, I wouldn't want Jack to think I'm not as funny as I used to be.

Now, on with the article. When the Teacher's people asked me— Hold it!

One night Benny Rubin was going to Jack's house for dinner, and I said to Benny Rubin, "If you want to have a little fun, make Jack a ten-dollar bet that if he calls me on the phone, I won't hang up on him."

Sure enough, that night my phone rang and it was Jack. We talked, and talked, and talked—oh, for about twenty minutes. Finally Jack couldn't stand it any longer. He said, "George, aren't you going to hang up on me?"

I said, "Why should I, I've got half of Benny Rubin's bet." That he didn't laugh at.

Well, I better stop talking about Jack Benny and start saying something nice about Teacher's Scotch. If you're dining at home or dining at a restaurant, the most sociable drink is Teacher's Scotch. Whether you're young, or whether you're old, Teacher's is the perfect scotch for any age. . . .

Age—that word keeps haunting me. People always want to know how old I am. They're always asking if I'm older than Jack Benny or if Jack Benny is older than me. I should settle it once and for all: I'm two years younger than Jack, and Jack is two years younger than Groucho Marx. I won't tell you our exact ages, but I will give you a little hint— Georgie Jessel, who is seventy-five years old, is the kid we send to run our errands.

Now back to Teacher's— Hold it! How do you like that, I'm finished. I wrote a whole article about Teacher's Scotch and never got to it!

The more I read this article the better I liked it. I really thought I had a very funny piece of material. In fact, I felt so enthused I drove over to Jack Benny's office to read it to him. Jack wasn't there, so I read it to his personal manager, Irving Fein, and when I had finished he said, "George, it's a very funny article. How much are they going to pay Jack for this?"

I said, "Irving, I wrote the article. Why should they pay Jack?"

"Because the whole thing is about him," Irving said. "If it wasn't for Jack, you wouldn't have an article." I couldn't argue with that. Irving continued, "George, I realize that you and Jack are very close, but I'm just being practical. When Jack Benny's name is used to promote a product, he gets paid an awful lot of money. It would be a minimum of twenty-five-thousand dollars."

Well, that made me stop and think. I said, "Irving, you're right. I'll write a whole new article and I won't even mention Jack's name."

As I got up to leave, Irving said, "George, I'm sorry you can't use that article you wrote. It's a shame it came out so funny."

I didn't bother to answer that line, I just left.

The next morning when I came into the office I said, "Fellows, we'll have to rewrite that whole Teacher's article."

Well, this brought moans and groans from Jack Langdon and Packy. Packy complained, "That's a very funny article. I can't see any reason to change it."

"You're right," I said. "But if we do the article the way it is, we have to give Jack Benny twenty-five-thousand dollars. So we'll have to split it three ways."

There wasn't a sound while that sank in. Then Packy said, "That's a damn good reason to change it."

Jack Langdon put a piece of paper in the typewriter and said, "Let's start the new article fast."

I said, "Good. And I've already thought of a title I think will work. There's a line I used to do in nightclubs, and if we just switch it a little, I think it'll make a great title."

That line I did was, "I love to sing. I'd rather sing than eat. And my friends who have heard me sing, would rather hear me eat." The boys and I switched the line, and here's the final title and the article that went with it:

I LOVE TO SING.
AND I LOVE TO DRINK SCOTCH.
MOST PEOPLE WOULD RATHER HEAR
ME DRINK SCOTCH.
By George Burns

When they asked me to write this article, they said to be sure and mention Teacher's Scotch, but not to drag it in, make it sound natural. Well, I just mentioned it, and that sounded natural. It sounded so natural I'll mention it again—Teacher's Scotch.

I'm a great writer. If I had a beard, I'd be another Hemingway.

They told me they wanted a fresh approach. Well, to write fresh you have to think fresh, and to think fresh you have to be fresh. I haven't been fresh January twentieth will be thirty-one years. I'm not going to tell you my age, but I've reached that point in life where I catch cold if I smoke a cigar without a holder on it.

But don't worry, I'll never give up singing. In fact, I started singing the day I was born. I remember the doctor kept slapping me, but I wouldn't stop until I finished two choruses of "Wait Till the Sun Shines, Nellie." And when I segued into the verse to "Honeysuckle Rose," he put me in the incubator and turned off the heat. It's a good thing I was smoking a cigar or I'd have froze to death.

I never did like that doctor. He wouldn't put Teacher's Scotch in my bottle.—See how naturally I mentioned that without dragging it in. I'm a great writer even without a beard. But I've found out that a little drink now and then helps my singing. It loosens my vocal cords. Sometimes my vocal cords get so loose that whenever I hit a low note I step on them. And when I step on them, I hit a high note. I lead a very nervous life. In the morning I get up a baritone, and when I go to bed I'm a soprano.

As you're reading this some of it may be funny, and then again some of it won't. So just read the funny stuff and skip the rest of it. But if the rest of it turns out to be the funny stuff, and the funny stuff turns out to be the rest of it, if I were you, I'd skip the funny stuff, too.

That last paragraph has so much rhythm you could almost dance to it. Well, I'll have another little sip of Teacher's Scotch, then back to the old typewriter. — How about that? — another natural mention. If I keep writing like this, I'll win the Pulitzer Prize.

Now that I've started it makes me mad after all these years to discover that something I've never done is what I do best. There may be hundreds of things I've never done that I'm great at. Tomorrow I'll take a crack at painting. I'll get a brush and some paint, and lie on my back and paint my bathroom ceiling. I may even make my own paint.

And if that works out, I'll paint the Mona Lisa. But in my version she'll have a reason to smile, because I'll have her holding a glass of Teacher's Scotch in her hand. — Another natural mention — and in oil, yet.

You know, there's an old saying which I just made up: "Don't do something that you can't do, and then do it." As soon as I get Mona out of the way, I'm going into a new project. I'll take up ballet dancing.

No, I better forget that. If I get up on my toes, I might step on my vocal cords again. I better stick to writing.

I find that writing is just like singing. But it's kind of hard to end an article with a yodeling finish. But you've got to have an ending, so here goes: I'm going to make this ending so subtle that you won't even notice I'm being natural.

Two men were standing at a bar. One was drinking Teacher's Scotch with his left hand, and the other was drinking Teacher's Scotch with his right hand. So I said to the one who was drinking Teacher's with his left hand, "Why do you drink Teacher's with your left hand?"

He said, "I always drink Teacher's with my left hand."

Then I said to the fellow who was drinking Teacher's with his right hand, "Why do you drink Teacher's with your right hand?"

He said, "Because if I didn't drink Teacher's with my right hand, you'd keep mistaking me for that fellow who drinks Teacher's with his left hand."

Well, that's the article, and I'm glad I wrote it. It's opened a whole new career for me. It turns out I write as good as I sing.

Well, the Teacher's people were ecstatic about it. The title with my picture appeared on billboards, and the article was published in all the top magazines and newspapers. At the height of the campaign I ran into Jack Benny at the Hillcrest Country Club. He said to me, "I just read that ad of yours in *Time* magazine."

"What'd you think of it?" I asked him.

"I've never been so hurt in my life," he said. "You're supposed to be my best friend, that article ran two full pages, and you didn't have the decency to mention my name!"

I said, "Sorry about that, Jack, you're too expensive to mention."

As Jack stared at me trying to figure out what I was talking about, I left for the card room.

Open-Heart Surgery Can Be Fun!

I came from a very large family. There were five brothers and seven sisters, and we were all healthy kids. My folks were so poor we couldn't afford to get sick.

When we were growing up we didn't worry about proteins, carbohydrates, vitamins, etc. We were happy with whatever my mother had in the pot. I still remember that pot. It was a big iron kettle that my mother kept cooking on the stove, and everything that came into the house went into that pot.

Now, feeding a family of fourteen with the few pennies my mother had to work with took a real genius. And that she was. Her secret was the sauce she always kept cooking in that pot. It was stove-hot and highly seasoned. She knew that anything she served under that sauce would taste good. You could put my mother's sauce on chipped wood and it would be delicious. In fact, I think one time I ate my brother Sammy's yo-yo.

I don't know if I owe it all to my mother's spicy sauce, but all my life I've enjoyed very good health. I've never allowed aches and pains to bother me. I just learned to live with them. There were times I didn't feel good, but no matter how bad I felt, show business came first. I'd go out on the stage, sing and dance and do my act, and then get ready for the next show. When you do five shows a day you forget anything was wrong with you in the first place.

When I was about twenty-one I was doing a song and dance act with a fellow named Billy Lorraine. We were on the Pantages circuit, and we were playing Minneapolis, when it became necessary for me to have my tonsils taken out. I found a doctor who would take care of me on a Sunday, which was our only day off, and it had to be done in the morning, because at two o'clock that afternoon Billy and I were catching the train to Vancouver. It was important that we catch that train, because if we didn't get to Vancouver in time for the matinee, we'd be canceled for the rest of the circuit.

That week I'd been going with a little usherette from the theater, and she offered to come up to the doctor's office with me. To show my appreciation I gave her a meal ticket I had from a local cafeteria which still had $3.20 worth of food unpunched on it. It wasn't that I was such a big sport, it was just that I knew that after I had my tonsils out I wouldn't be able to eat anyway.

Well, we got to the doctor's office at ten o'clock that morning, and by ten thirty my tonsils were out.

The doctor said to me, "You better rest here for about three hours, and then go home and stay in bed for two days."

I could barely talk, but I managed to whisper, "Doctor, I can't do that, I'm catching a train for Vancouver at two o'clock and I'm doing a matinee tomorrow at noon."

The doctor couldn't believe what he heard. He said, "That's impossible—you're liable to hemorrhage."

"Then I'll take the tonsils with me," I said, "and if I hemorrhage, I'll put them back in."

There was nothing he could do, so at one thirty I was all packed and standing in front of the hotel waiting to leave for the train. In a few minutes Billy Lorraine met me.

"Did you have your tonsils taken out?" he asked me.

I nodded yes and opened my mouth. Billy took one look and fainted right on the spot.

By the time we got to Vancouver I was so weak I could hardly stand up, and my voice was even worse. I told the theater manager that Billy Lorraine would have to work

40

alone that day, but I'd be ready the next. Well, when Billy and I worked together we were not one of the great two-acts—we were just plain bad. And when Billy went out there alone doing half of a bad act, he was lucky he got off alive.

Anyway, the manager was furious. He ran into our dressing room and shouted, "Look, Burns, if both of you aren't out on that stage for the next show, the act is canceled!"

The next show I was out there. What could I do? I wanted to stay in show business. But as it worked out, it helped my entire career. From that performance on I stopped singing tenor and started singing the way I do today.

Now, I don't know whether you've heard me sing or not. I like the way I sing—I love the way I sing. I wouldn't go so far as to say I'm the greatest singer in show business, however. There are plenty of fellows who sing better than I do; there's Frank Sinatra, Tony Bennett, and that's it.

I'll let you in on something—it's a lot easier for me to work in a theater than it is for them. Guys like Sinatra and Bennett need special lighting effects, great musical arrangements, and they carry the top musicians. Their exits are very important because when they exit they need applause to bring them back. Not me. I don't have that problem; I don't exit. I just stay there and finish my songs. Sometimes the audience exits. But that doesn't phase me. As long as I'm there I know somebody loves me.

But as I was saying before I rudely interrupted myself, after having my tonsils taken out I didn't see a doctor again for the next twenty years. And oddly enough, when I did have to see one it was my throat again. I had developed sort of a tickle in my throat which caused me to constantly keep clearing it. It got so I couldn't even finish a sentence without doing it. By then I was married to Gracie, and with all this hacking of mine she couldn't get any sleep. Also, we were on radio at the time, so I was not only annoying Gracie, I was annoying the whole country.

Anyway, I went to all the great doctors, every throat specialist I could find. They all looked into my throat and said the same thing—"Stop smoking!" So I stopped, and it got worse.

One day Abe Lastfogel called me—he was the head of the William Morris Agency—and said, "George, I heard you on the radio last night, and you better do something about that throat. If you keep hacking that way, the sponsor's never going to renew your contract."

I said, "Abe, I don't know what to do. I've been to every doctor in the country."

"George," Abe said, "you haven't been to Dr. Ginsberg. He runs a little eye, ear, nose and throat clinic in downtown Los Angeles. He only charges three dollars a visit and he's a genius."

Well, I got down there as fast as I could. When I went into his office there were about forty people in the waiting room. I went over to the nurse and said, "Would you tell Dr. Ginsberg that George Burns is sitting outside."

She went into the other office, and a minute later she returned. She said, "I told Dr. Ginsberg that George Burns was sitting outside, and he told me to tell you that Dr. Ginsberg is sitting inside." So I sat down, hacked, coughed, cleared my throat and waited my turn.

When I finally got into the doctor's office I kept hacking, and hacking, and hacking. He examined my throat and said, "What's your problem?"

I said, "What's my problem! Can't you tell? I keep making this hacking noise."

The doctor said, "Why do you do that?"

I sat there stunned. Nobody had ever asked me that question before. I said, "I don't know why I do it."

Dr. Ginsberg said, "Then if I were you, I wouldn't do it anymore."

And you know something—I never did.

I paid my $3, and as I started to leave I turned to the doctor and said, "Doctor, aren't you going to give me something to take?"

He opened a drawer and took out a box of jelly beans. "I usually give these to children," he said, "but since you're such a big star, I'll give you one of the black ones."

Anyway, I stopped hacking, Gracie was able to sleep again, Abe Lastfogel was happy, the sponsor renewed our contract, and I was hooked on black jelly beans.

After that I enjoyed perfect health until 1947. So let's jump ahead ten years. It's easy for me to jump ahead in this book, but in real life I don't want to jump ahead ten seconds—what am I talking about, make that five.

By 1947 Gracie and I were established radio stars, and one day my agent called and told me our sponsor had just picked up our option for another season. In those days when you were picked up it wasn't just for thirteen weeks, it was for thirty-nine weeks with thirteen weeks of repeats. This meant fifty-two full weeks of very big money. Well, naturally I was excited, and I couldn't wait to rush home to tell Gracie.

When I got to the house it was midmorning, and Gracie's favorite pastime was listening to those soap operas on the radio—and that's what she was doing. I came in all out of breath and said, "Gracie, I've got marvelous news!"

She put her finger to her lips and said, "Shhh, not now, George—Ma Perkins is in trouble."

So I had to sit there and wait for fifteen minutes until Ma Perkins got out of trouble. Finally, when it was over, I said, "Gracie, the sponsors just picked up our option and we're signed for another fifty-two weeks!"

She smiled. "That's wonderful," she said. "Isn't it nice that Ma Perkins and I got good news on the same day!"

"Gracie," I said, "it's a fifty-two-week deal. Don't you want to know how much money we'll be making?"

"Of course, but you can tell me later, George. Right now Our Gal Sunday is coming on."

That evening we were going out to celebrate, and while Gracie was upstairs getting dressed I went behind the bar to make myself a martini. As I turned to reach for the vermouth, suddenly I fainted. I was only out for a few seconds, and when I came to I felt just fine. I also felt a little silly. When you've just signed a contract for fifty-two weeks, that's no time to faint. Fainting is for actors who are laying off. Anyway, I decided not to even mention it to anybody. Gracie and I went out that night to celebrate, and I forgot about it.

A couple of nights later Gracie was upstairs, and I wanted to ask her something. I went over to the stairs, looked up and called her, and just like that I fainted again. When Gracie came down there I was lying on the floor. In another few seconds I was fine again, but Gracie was all upset. When I told her about fainting before she said, "George, I don't want any arguments, you're going to see Dr. Kennamer first thing in the morning."

The next day, in Dr. Kennamer's office, I told him my story. He listened to the whole thing and then asked me, "George, when you reached for the gin to make your martini which way did you turn?"

I said, "I turned to the right."

"When you went to call Gracie which way did you turn?"

"To the right."

"Sit up on the table here, George," he said. "I want to see if I can make you faint." He pressed something behind my right ear, and I fainted. When I came to, he said, "George, what you've got is an exposed nerve. The next time you make a martini or call Gracie, turn to the left."

His advice was perfect. It never bothered me again. Dr. Kennamer reminded me a lot of Dr. Ginsberg. The only difference was he didn't give me a black jelly bean and he charged me a lot more than $3.

For the next twenty-seven years healthwise, the worst thing that happened to me was a badly chapped lower lip. Things had been going too well, and I figured that sooner or later something was bound to happen. And when I got to be seventy-eight years old it did. I noticed that every so often I'd experience pains in my chest. I don't remember how

44

long this went on, but the pains started to come more often. However, that didn't bother me because at my age I like a little pain once in a while—at least I know I'm alive.

Anyway, it turned out that I had to be operated on. Now I don't think you'd be interested in a long, dull medical description of my operation, so I've thought of a better way to tell it. You may not believe this, but three months after the operation I was feeling great and went on the Johnny Carson show and told all about it. Now this isn't exactly the way it happened, but when you're working with Johnny Carson you better get a few laughs. (But one little reminder; as you read this keep in mind that my good friend Jack Benny was still with us at the time.)

Now, I'm just telling you what I said. If Johnny wants to tell you what he said, let him write his own book. All right, on November 13, 1974, after Johnny Carson introduced me, here's how it went:

Thank you, Johnny. Well, here I am, right from the operating table at Cedars of Lebanon to *The Tonight Show*. I'm very glad to be here . . . in fact, I'm glad to be anyplace. . . .

But that operation I had, how that happened was pretty crazy. You see, Johnny, I had been getting these pains in my chest, and I couldn't figure out what was causing them. Then I got a bright idea. Maybe it was because I wasn't wearing a vest—so I started wearing a vest. But then I started getting pains in my left arm, and I thought maybe my cigars were too heavy—so I started smoking with my right hand. There I was, wearing a vest and smoking with my right hand, but the pains were still there. . . .

I didn't think anything more about it until a few days later at Hillcrest when I was playing bridge the pains started up again. Now, I was holding a very good hand—an opening two bid with 150 honors in hearts. If I could feel the pain while I was holding a hand like that, I knew I was in trouble. . . . I had another member play my hand, and I went right to my doctors, Dr. Rex Kennamer and Dr. Gary Sugarman.

45

After they examined me, Dr. Kennamer said, "George, this is serious."

I said, "Whatever you have to do, do it fast. I want to get back to the club, the guy playing my hand is a lousy bridge player."

He looked real serious and said, "George, you're going to have to go to the hospital."

"Okay," I said, "let's book it for next week."

He shook his head and said, "George, you've got to go right now."

"What about my bridge game?" I asked him.

He looked straight at me and said, "George, if you don't go now, you may never play bridge again."

I couldn't believe what I had just heard. I said, "Is it that serious?"

Dr. Sugarman put his hand on my shoulder and said, "George, I hate to be this blunt, but if you don't go now, you could die."

I'd never died before, but somehow I didn't think I would like it— Oh, come to think of it, I died in New Haven, Schenectady, and Altoona, but this kind of dying could cancel you out of show business.

Anyway, when I got to the hospital Dr. Kennamer told me they were going to do open-heart surgery; take some veins out of my leg and bypass some arteries in my heart. I didn't know what he was talking about. I said, "Look, doctor, whatever you have to do, do it, but make sure you don't touch my vocal cords, because that's how I make my living."

Well, they gave me some pills that made me very groggy and took me downstairs. The doctor said, "George, we're going to put some fluid into your system and show you exactly what we're going to do. And you can watch yourself on that television screen."

Johnny, can I tell you something—I looked lousy. I had no makeup on.

When the test was over, Dr. Kennamer said, "Well, George, that's what we're gonna do," and I said, "Well, do it fast, because that thing I just saw on the screen is not going to play Las Vegas."

That afternoon they operated on me. I was on the table for

46

about five or six hours, and then they put me in the Intensive Care Unit. When I came to, the first thing I did was sing "The Red Rose Rag." I wanted to make sure my vocal cords were still there.

Anyway, Johnny, my operation was a tremendous success. Dr. Kennamer and Dr. Sugarman handled the whole thing, and they're the greatest. Dr. Jack Matloff's cardiac team operated on me, and they were great. The operation was done at Cedars of Lebanon Hospital, which is also great. So because of those great people, Johnny, here I am feeling great.

And there isn't anything I did before the operation that I can't do again. That means I can do nothing. . . . I did nothing before the operation and I can do nothing now. . . . And if you don't believe me, ask Trixie Hart . . . or Lilly LaMott . . . or Glenda Gibson . . . or Betty DeFore . . . I did nothing with a lot of girls. . . .

But naturally, Johnny, an operation like that has a big effect on your life. But don't get me wrong, I never felt better, but Dr. Kennamer did foul up my eating habits. Johnny, no ketchup . . . I put ketchup on everything. Me without ketchup is like Dean Martin splitting a milk shake with Phil Harris. . . .

Another thing—no salt. For breakfast I've always had scrambled eggs with a lot of ketchup and a lot of salt. Now I've gotta eat them just plain. Johnny, did you know eggs were yellow? You know, I'm seventy-eight years old and I've had eggs all my life, and I never knew they tasted like that . . . sort of a nothing taste . . . kind of bland. They taste like the chicken wasn't getting paid. . . .

But now I have to go every week to Dr. Kennamer's office for a checkup. And, Johnny, you're not going to believe what happened to me while I was waiting there last week—

There was a woman sitting there, and after looking at me for a minute or so she said, "It's exciting to be sitting in a waiting room with a celebrity."

I said, "Yes, it is exciting. Who are you?" She kind of laughed, and said, "I mean you. I watch you all the time, I'm a big fan of yours. By the way, how's your wife Mary?"

"Mary's just fine," I answered, "she was fine when I left her in bed this morning."

47

"That stingy character you play," the woman said. "You're not that way in real life, are you?"

I said, "Of course not."

Then she said something I couldn't believe my ears. She said, "Mr. Benny, is it true that everything George Burns says makes you laugh?"

"Oh, yes," I said, "he's one of the funniest men in show business. I wish I had his sense of humor."

She said, "I like George Burns, too, and I watch him all the time. How come he never finishes a song?"

"Well, he's reached the age now where he can't finish anything anymore," I said. Then I added, "What's your name?" And she said, "Mrs. Schwartz."

"Mrs. Schwartz," I said, "listen to this—

(*sings*)

  Down in the garden where the red roses grow,
  Oh my, I long to go
  Pluck me like a flower,
  Cuddle me an hour,
  Lovie, let me learn that red rose rag . . .

"Whom does that sound like?"

Mrs. Schwartz said, "George Burns—but, Mr. Benny, Rich Little does a better imitation of him than you do."

Then the nurse came out and said, "The doctor will see you now, Mr. Burns."

Mrs. Schwartz's mouth fell open a bit, and she said, "Mr. Burns! Are you George Burns?"

"That's right," I said.

And very indignantly she said, "Well, what were you doing in bed with Mary this morning?!"

I said, "At our age it takes both Jack and myself to keep her warm. Good-bye Mrs. Schwartz."

Well, that's the way I told it on *The Johnny Carson Show*. Isn't that better than going into a lot of grim detail? Sure, I knew it was a serious operation, but I didn't allow myself to get uptight about it. That just happens to be the

48

kind of person I am. I had the finest doctors I could get, I was in a hospital with all the latest equipment, so what more could I do about it—it was out of my hands. I was fortunate, because ten years ago this bypass operation had never been heard of, and today it's very successful. So the point is, nobody should ever give up hope. Every day medical science is developing new cures for practically everything.

That's about all I'm going to say about my operation. And for you skeptics who doubt that my vocal cords came through unscathed, some night if you're giving a sociable at your house, invite me over. I'll bring my piano player and sing twenty or thirty songs for you. And if you haven't got a piano, I'll bring that, too.

Gracie and Me

I was married to Gracie for thirty-eight years, and it was a marvelous marriage. It worked. Now don't get me wrong, we had arguments, but not like other couples had. Our arguments were never about our marriage. When we had a disagreement, it had to do with show business. I know that it's a common belief among many psychologists and marriage counselors that you can't mix marriage with a career. Well, I've got news for them—they can mix, and Gracie and I proved it for thirty-eight years.

An average couple who has been married for thirty-eight years are with each other for about six hours a day. This means they see each other about one fourth of the time, so in thirty-eight years of marriage they've only been together a little over nine years.

But not Gracie and me. We got up together, we dressed together, we ate together, we worked together, we played together, we were together twenty-four hours a day. That meant in thirty-eight years of marriage Gracie and I were together four times longer than the average couple.

(I hope my fifth grade teacher, Miss Hollander, reads this. She flunked me once in arithmetic.)

You know, lots of times people have asked me what Gracie and I did to make our marriage work. It's simple—we didn't do anything. I think the trouble with a lot of people is that they work too hard at staying married. They make a business out of it. When you work too hard at a business you get tired; and when you get tired you get grouchy; and when you get grouchy you start fighting; and when you start fighting you're out of business.

(I'm another Dear Abby.)

Looking back, I really don't know why Gracie married me. I certainly know why I wanted to marry her. She was a living Irish doll; such a dainty little thing, only 102 pounds, with long, blue-black hair and sparkling eyes; so full of life, and with an infectious laugh that made her fun to be around. Besides all that she was a big talent; she could sing, she was a great dancer, and a fine actress with a marvelous flair for comedy.

But why did she marry me? As they say in music, I was tacit. I was nothing. I was already starting to lose my hair, I had a voice like a frog, I stuttered and stammered, I was a bad, small-time vaudeville actor and I was broke. I guess she must have felt sorry for me.

I'm glad she did.

I'm not going to tell you about meeting Gracie—our courtship—my proposal—or that $17 wedding ring I gave her that was marked down to $11. I've told those stories over and over again. But there is one incident that I'd like to repeat. I don't know if you'll enjoy it, but when this book comes out, I'd like to read it again.

When I first started working with Gracie she was going with a fellow named Benny Ryan. Now, Benny Ryan was in love with Gracie, I was in love with Gracie, and Gracie was in love with Benny Ryan. Benny never got jealous about Gracie working with me, because in his mind I was no competition. As far as he was concerned Gracie could have been working with a trained seal.

There was no way I could compete with Benny Ryan. He was not only a charming, witty Irishman, but he had a tremendous talent. He was considered one of our great dancers, he wrote comedy sketches for some of the biggest stars, and he was a very successful songwriter. To show you what a great sense of humor he had, one of the songs he wrote

52

was called "When Frances Dances with Me," and this was the closing couplet:

> She does a new step,
> It goes one, two, three, kick;
> She can't count so good,
> That's the worst of the trick.
> My shin bones look like they've
> Been hit with a brick
> When Frances dances with me.

How could I compete with a guy who could write a lyric like that? I always thought that "moon" rhymed with "January."

Anyway, here I was in love with this lovely girl and I knew I didn't stand a chance with her. But as I said, every time I would hit bottom something always happened that made me bounce back. Well, I bounced.

Gracie and I were booked to play eighteen weeks on the Orpheum Circuit. This was big-time vaudeville and involved a tour of all the major cities in the Western states. The day before we were set to leave, Benny Ryan arrived back in town. When he heard about our tour he asked Gracie to cancel the tour and marry him. But as much as Gracie was in love with Benny Ryan, she was too nice a person to walk out on me with such short notice. She knew how important it was for me to play these big-time theaters, so she told Benny he would just have to wait until we returned from the tour, and then she'd marry him. Benny was furious, but I was bouncing again. I figured if I had eighteen weeks on the road with Gracie anything could happen.

The team of Burns & Allen was making $400 a week, which meant $200 for each of us. Out of that I had to pay commission to my agent, send money home to my mother, pay my railroad fares, my hotel bills, and my food. So this left me with about $85 a week, and I was spending every

53

nickel of it trying to make an impression on Gracie. Wherever we were on the tour I'd take her to dinner at the best restaurant in town, and when we were through working at night I'd often take her dancing at the finest hotels.

Well, after nine weeks we landed in San Francisco. I was still nowhere and I was broke. Now, you wouldn't think a case of appendicitis would play a big part in a romance, but in my case it did. We were playing the Orpheum Theater in San Francisco, and in the middle of the week Gracie was rushed to the hospital for an emergency appendectomy. Before she went into surgery she asked me to wire Benny Ryan in New York and let him know she was in the hospital. I sent the wire, but believe me, my heart wasn't in it—and besides that, it cost me my last seventy-five cents. It was not one of my bright moments.

Anyway, Gracie came through the operation fine, but while she recovered it meant that I had to stay in San Francisco for three weeks with no money coming in. Gracie knew this, and she said to me, "George, my mother lives here in San Francisco, and I've arranged for you to stay with her until I can go back to work." And as if that wasn't enough, she also knew I was broke, so she loaned me $200 to get by on.

Well, there I was—I had a place to stay, home cooking, and $200 in my pocket. You'd think I'd be happy—but I wasn't. All I could think of was that telegram she had me send to Benny Ryan.

Of course, I was at the hospital every day, and after about four or five days I noticed Gracie was very upset. Finally she came out and said, "I can't understand it. I haven't heard a word from Benny Ryan since we left New York. You'd think he'd at least send flowers when he knows I'm in the hospital." Then she looked at me and said, "George, are you sure you sent that telegram?"

I said, "Yes, Gracie, I sent it. I didn't want to, but I sent it."

When I left the hospital that day I still had $160—and the beginning of a brainstorm. I went to the nearest florist and sent Gracie $160 worth of flowers—all sorts of flowers, every kind of flower I had ever heard of. Now, in those days $160 worth of flowers not only filled Gracie's room but that hospital had flowers coming out all the windows.

But it worked! The next day, after fighting my way through the flowers to Gracie's bedside, she gave me a big smile and said, "George, anybody who would spend my two hundred dollars to send me flowers has to be a very nice man." And then she kissed me. In my mind's eye I could see Benny Ryan bite the dust.

Anyway, after the tour Gracie and I were married. And now that I look back, I don't think I ever paid her back that $200.

During the first year of our marriage everything worked. Our marriage was a success, careerwise we were doing well, our salaries were getting better—everything was getting better except me on the stage. I was still pathetic. I did absolutely nothing and put on makeup to do it. Fortunately, it didn't matter that I wasn't improving, because Gracie was so good she carried both of us.

I'll never forget the first time we were booked into the Palace Theater in New York. It was a very exciting break for us; playing the Palace was the goal of every vaudeville act in the country.

Just try to imagine two young performers being booked into the top vaudeville theater in the nation and knowing that when they walked out onstage for the opening matinee the theater would be packed with actors, critics, and bookers. Thinking about it made both of us nervous wrecks.

Gracie bought herself a brand-new outfit from head to toes, and I had my spats cleaned. The night before we opened I really went all out. I bought a couple of bottles of champagne because I thought all our friends would be coming up to our hotel room to celebrate our opening; people like Blossom Seeley, Benny Fields, Mary Kelly, Tom Swift, Jack and Mary Benny, Orry Kelly, and Archibald Leach. (He later went into pictures. I think he changed his name to Cary Grant.)

Well, we sat there waiting for a couple of hours, but nobody showed up. Finally I picked up the phone and called Jack Benny. I said, "Jack, where is everybody? I even bought some champagne because I thought you'd all be by to have a drink and help us celebrate."

Jack said, "George, we're all over here at my place. We were gonna come by, but then we talked it over. We decided since you and Gracie are opening at the Palace tomorrow night it would be better if you got some rest."

After I hung up, Gracie said, "George, what are we going to do with this champagne?" With that I opened a bottle. We both had a drink and Gracie went to bed. I didn't want that bottle of champagne to go flat, so I stayed up an extra hour. You know something? It's impossible to get a champagne cork back into the bottle.

The next thing we knew we were backstage in our dressing room putting on our makeup. There was no conversation between us. Gracie was so nervous it took her three different tries before she could get her lips on right. But for some strange reason I was as cool as a cucumber. I finally did figure it out. When you go on the stage and don't do anything, there's very little to get nervous about.

Well, the big moment finally arrived! There we were, standing in the wings of the Palace Theater, ready to go on! I took Gracie's hand, our music started to play, we made our entrance, and this is the act we did the very first time we played the Palace:

(Play-on music:)
   (George and Gracie enter holding hands. Gracie stops, turns, looks toward the wings, and waves. She lets go of George's hand and walks toward the wing, still waving. Then she stops and beckons to whomever she is waving to

56

come out. A man comes out, puts his arms around Gracie, and kisses her, and she kisses him. They wave to each other as he backs offstage. Gracie returns to George center stage.)

GRACIE

Who was that?

GEORGE

You don't know?

GRACIE

No, my mother told me never to talk to strangers.

GEORGE

That makes sense.

GRACIE

This always happens to me. On my way in, a man stopped me at the stage door and said, "Hiya, cutie, how about a bite tonight after the show?"

GEORGE

And you said?

GRACIE

I said, "I'll be busy after the show but I'm not doing anything now," so I bit him.

GEORGE

Gracie, let me ask you something. Did the nurse ever happen to drop you on your head when you were a baby?

GRACIE

Oh, no, we couldn't afford a nurse, my mother had to do it.

GEORGE

You had a smart mother.

GRACIE

Smartness runs in my family. When I went to school I was so smart my teacher was in my class for five years.

GEORGE

Gracie, what school did you go to?

57

GRACIE
I'm not allowed to tell.

GEORGE
Why not?

GRACIE
The school pays me $25 a month not to tell.

GEORGE
Is there anybody in the family as smart as you?

GRACIE
My sister Hazel is even smarter. If it wasn't for her, our canary would never have hatched that ostrich egg.

GEORGE
A canary hatched an ostrich egg?

GRACIE
Yeah . . . but the canary was too small to cover that big egg.

GEORGE
So?

GRACIE
So . . . Hazel sat on the egg and held the canary in her lap.

GEORGE
Hazel must be the smartest in your family.

GRACIE
Oh, no. My brother Willy was no dummy either.

GEORGE
Willy?

GRACIE
Yeah, the one who slept on the floor.

GEORGE
Why would he sleep on the floor?

GRACIE
He had high blood pressure—

58

GEORGE
And he was trying to keep it down?

GRACIE
Yeah.

GEORGE
I'd like to meet Willy.

GRACIE
You can't miss him. He always wears a high collar to cover the appendicitis scar on his neck.

GEORGE
Gracie, your appendix is down around your waist.

GRACIE
I know, but Willy was so ticklish they had to operate up there.

GEORGE
What's Willy doing now?

GRACIE
He just lost his job.

GEORGE
Lost his job?

GRACIE
Yeah, he's a window washer.

GEORGE
And?

GRACIE
And . . . he was outside on the twentieth story washing a window and when he got through he stepped back to admire his work.

GEORGE
And he lost his job.

GRACIE
Yeah . . . And when he hit the pavement he was terribly embarrassed.

GEORGE

Embarrassed?

GRACIE

Yeah . . . his collar flew off and his appendicitis scar showed.

GEORGE

Gracie, this family of yours—

GRACIE

When Willy was a little baby my father took him riding in his carriage, and two hours later my father came back with a different baby and a different carriage.

GEORGE

Well, what did your mother say?

GRACIE

My mother didn't say anything because it was a better carriage.

GEORGE

A better carriage?

GRACIE

Yeah . . . And the little baby my father brought home was a little French baby so my mother took up French.

GEORGE

Why?

GRACIE

So she would be able to understand the baby—

GEORGE

When the baby started to talk?

GRACIE

Yeah.

GEORGE

Gracie, this family of yours, do you all live together?

GRACIE

Oh, sure. My father, my brother, my uncle, my cousin and my nephew all sleep in one bed and—

In one bed? I'm surprised your grandfather doesn't sleep with them.

Oh, he did, but he died, so they made him get up.

Well, those were the jokes Gracie and I told at the Palace, and looking back at them I still think they're pretty funny. But as I said before, Gracie was the act. I think you'll agree when you take another look at the hilarious lines I had. I said:

—"You don't know?"
—"So?"
—"And?"
—"Well, what did your mother say?"
—"When the baby started to talk?"

And those were the kind of lines that made me a star.

Following this comedy routine the lights would come down and a spotlight would hit Gracie while she sang a song. The audience loved her because her voice had a beautiful quality, pure and delightful. During this I stood over to one side in the dark. Many critics thought this was the high point of my performance.

And Gracie was a marvelous Irish clog dancer. So at the end of her song the music would segue into this very fast Irish jig, which Gracie danced to. Every part of her body went into that dance. Her feet were lightning quick and she never missed a tap. She created such excitement that at the end of her dance it brought down the house. Then the lights would come up, and while Gracie was bowing I stood there applauding her.

After the applause died down we continued with our act. This consisted of about ten more minutes of comedy dialogue, which was very easy for me because all I had to do was repeat those lines I did in the first part.

Our act ended with a typical boy-girl song, which led into the both of us dancing together. During this dance we used a gimmick which I think I originated. It's been used many times over the years—in fact, it's still being used and it still works. Gracie and I would dance together, and four times during the number I would stop the music—we would tell a joke—and then continue dancing. It went like this:

(George and Gracie go into dance)

GEORGE

Stop!
(Music stops)
Gracie, how is your cousin?

GRACIE

You mean the one who died?

GEORGE

Yeah.

GRACIE

Oh, he's fine now.

GEORGE

Music!
(Music starts, and dance continues)

GEORGE

Stop!
(Music stops)
Gracie, how's your uncle Harvey?

GRACIE

Oh, last night he fell down the stairs with a bottle of scotch and never spilled a drop.

GEORGE

Really?

GRACIE

Yeah, he kept his mouth closed.

Music!
(Music starts, and dance continues)

GEORGE

Stop!
(Music stops)

GRACIE

My sister Bessie had a brand new-baby.

GEORGE

Boy or girl?

GRACIE

I don't know, and I can't wait to get home to find out if I'm an aunt or an uncle.

GEORGE

Music!
(Music starts, and dance continues)

GEORGE

Stop!
(Music stops)
A funny thing happened to my mother in Cleveland.

GRACIE

I thought you were born in Buffalo.

GEORGE

Music!
(Music up—and into dancing exit)

Well, that was the routine Gracie and I did the first time at the Palace. And we were really a big hit. I know, I was there.

It's Fun To Look Back—If There Isn't Something Cuter in Front of You!

Now that I'm eighty I find that I have a lot in common with other people my age. There is still one thing we can all do—and we can do it standing up . . . lying down . . . sitting down . . . we can do it in any position. In fact, we can do it and drink a glass of water at the same time.

You know what it is? Being able to look back and reminisce! I'll bet you thought of a more exciting answer. Well, so did I, but this book is meant for family entertainment.

You know, most people when they look back they talk about what they would do if they could live their lives over again; how they wouldn't do this and they wouldn't do that, they'd change this and they'd change that, and all of the things they should have done differently. I've never had that problem. In all my years I've never made one mistake. Well, that's not true—on January 6, 1924, at two o'clock I made one mistake—no, I made two mistakes—look, I've made a lot of mistakes, but it never worried me. I'm glad I made all those mistakes. If it wasn't for them, when I go on the Johnny Carson or the Merv Griffin shows I wouldn't have anything to talk about. I even made a lot of those mistakes on purpose. I knew eventually Johnny Carson and Merv Griffin would grow up and have their own talk shows.

But there's nothing wrong with looking back. I know I do it, and I enjoy it. But I also enjoy looking to the future. The future I'm looking forward to tonight is about twenty-two years old and she's coming to my house for dinner. She's a beautiful little airline stewardess. We made a deal; I'm going to teach her how to sing and she's going to teach me how to fly. I'm not sure, but I think it's going to be easier for me to teach her to sing. But if this little girl can teach me to fly, it may mean a whole new chapter.

Look, I know I poke fun at everything, including myself, but that's been my philosophy all my life. I've always been able to laugh at my own problems. You'll find that most everyday little problems can be solved with laughter. For instance, if a man comes home and finds his wife making love to someone else, he should use my philosophy—don't get mad, just laugh. If it's a cold day, he could open the window so the other guy will catch cold.

Now, I may have exaggerated a bit that having a sense of humor helps get you through rough spots, but it does. I've observed that most people just take themselves too seriously, and if they do have a problem, once it's over they won't let go of it. I have actor friends who have been big stars for years. They still make fabulous salaries, they're happily married and have beautiful families, they live in magnificent homes with fine paintings on the walls, swimming pools, tennis courts, two or three cars, a staff of servants—anything money can buy. But even with all this luxury they're still bugged because during their careers they may have received three bad notices and those notices are still on their minds.

Even today I don't worry about reviews. If I get a bad review, I figure it's the reviewer who's bad, not me. If he doesn't like me, I don't have to like him. After all, we don't have to go dancing together.

When Gracie and I first started, we were playing in Oklahoma City one time and the morning after we opened there was a review of our act in the paper. This was what the man had to say in the last paragraph of his review:

   . . . Number Four on the Orpheum bill was a man and woman act, George Burns and Gracie Allen. Miss Allen is not only a beautiful young lady, but a great talent. She captivated the audience with her lovely voice, her exciting dancing, and her all-around stage presence. On top of all this her comedy timing is flawless. There is no telling how far Miss Allen could go if she worked alone.

Reading this didn't help my ego, but what could I do about it? I admit I wondered what Gracie's reaction would be, so after the show that night I borrowed ten dollars from her and invited her out to dinner. I took her to the nicest place in town. We had a drink, a crabmeat cocktail, and right in the middle of her lamb chops I said, "Gracie, what did you think of that notice in the paper this morning?"

She looked up at me, smiled sweetly, and said, "George, pass the salt."

So I passed her the salt. I was good at it, too, because I passed Gracie an awful lot of salt.

Now, all through this book I've been telling you how bad I was, so I imagine you're saying to yourselves if he was that bad, how did the team of Burns & Allen ever make it? Well, it's true I was bad, but only onstage. Offstage was something else again. I knew show business, especially vaudeville. I knew all the ingredients involved in putting an act together; I knew exits, entrances, how to construct a joke, how to switch a joke, where the laughs were going to drop, how to build an act to a strong finish. And most important, I knew the zany, off-center character Gracie Allen played onstage. I discovered the most effective way for Gracie to get laughs was by having her tell jokes that had what I called "illogical logic"; they sounded like they made sense, but they only made sense to Gracie. This tickled the audience and they fell in love with her because her honest delivery made all this unbelievable nonsense sound believable. So when I said to Gracie, "How's your brother?" and she went into five minutes of telling me, there was a lot of me in what she said.

As time went on I got better onstage. I had to. For me there was no way to go but up. My timing got better, I got more confidence in myself, and I learned how to keep out of Gracie's way so the audience would concentrate on her. I improved so much I finally got so good that nobody knew I was there.

By now Gracie and I were considered a big-time vaudeville act and we played nothing but the best theaters. We were in the third year of a five-year contract with the Keith-Orpheum circuit, and we played on the same bill with stars like Nora Bayes, Belle Baker, Eddie Cantor, Sophie Tucker, Blossom Seeley, you name them.

I was on cloud nine. In my wildest dreams I had never expected to get to this point in show business. And to top all that, here I was married to a wonderful girl who was not only marvelous onstage, but the perfect wife off. Well—not exactly perfect. Let me tell you a little personal secret about Gracie. She was everything a man could want in a wife, but her Irish background made her a very determined person. If she thought she was right about something, she wouldn't budge. Let me tell you a little something about what happened in New Orleans. This was before we were married, but it will give you an idea of what I'm talking about.

Gracie had bought a new dress, which cost her $400, to wear in our act. For her this was a very, very expensive dress, and she had saved for a long time to be able to afford it. Before we opened in New Orleans she sent the dress to a place called the Chiffon Cleaners, and when it came back the dress was ruined. It was a red and white dress and all the colors had run together and it was a mess. Naturally, when Gracie saw what they'd done she was heartbroken and went directly to the cleaners and demanded $400 to replace the dress. Well, she got nowhere. They claimed they weren't responsible and refused to do anything about it.

That afternoon in our dressing room before the matinee Gracie never said a word; she wouldn't even discuss the dress. But I could feel that her Irish was starting to bubble.

Anyway, we were on the stage doing our act, the theater was packed, and the audience was loving us. When we got to our closing number we came to the joke where I stopped the music and said, "A funny thing happened to my mother in Cleveland," and Gracie was supposed to answer, "I thought you were born in Buffalo." Well, instead of answering me, she just walked right down to the footlights and matter-of-factly said, "Ladies and gentlemen, when I arrived in New Orleans I had a brand new dress which cost me four hundred dollars, and yesterday for the first time I sent it to be cleaned by the Chiffon Cleaners, which is located at the corner of St. Charles and Canal Street. When it came back it was absolutely ruined. I immediately went down there, and since I could never wear the dress again, I asked them to make good on it. They not only refused, but they were very rude to me. The reason I'm telling you this, I'll be leaving New Orleans at the end of the week, but you people live here. So I'm warning you, don't send your clothes to the Chiffon Cleaners, which is located at the corner of St. Charles and Canal Street." And with that she turned and walked back to me, and said, "I thought you were born in Buffalo." Needless to say, that joke did not get a laugh. Not only was Gracie's dress ruined, but so was that joke.

That night, during our performance, she made the same speech, but in a different part of our act. I don't have to tell you, I was a nervous wreck. We still had six more days in New Orleans and I knew there was no way of stopping Gracie. The next day, when we arrived at the theater, the only thing I could think of was, When will she do it today? Will it be the same place as last night or yesterday afternoon? When? But fortunately for my peace of mind, there was an envelope for Gracie at the stage door with $400 in it, compliments of the Chiffon Cleaners, which was located at the corner of St. Charles and Canal Street.

When Gracie had something to say she got right to the point. Let me tell you something else that actually happened onstage. One time I came up with a joke that I thought would be perfect in our closing routine. I thought it was a very funny joke, so before the matinee I told it to Gracie. I said, "When I stop the music I'll say, 'What are you doing tonight?' And you say, 'I can't see you tonight, I'm expecting a headache.'"

She shook her head and said, "I don't like it. I don't think it's funny."

I said, "Gracie, I think it's a funny joke!"

She shook her head again and said, "I don't."

Trying to reason with her, I said, "Gracie, we'll leave it to the audience to decide. If they laugh at the joke, it's in, and if they don't, we'll take it out."

She shook her head and said, "It's not funny."

Well, Gracie wanted the joke out and I wanted it in. I'm not Irish, but I've got something that bubbles a little, too. At the matinee, when we came to that bit, I stopped the music and said, "Gracie, what are you doing tonight?" She just stood there, looked at me, and never said a word. I waited through about fifteen seconds of dead silence, then finally said, "Music," and we started dancing again.

I knew that sooner or later one of us would have to outbubble the other. For two weeks at every performance I said to Gracie, "What are you doing tonight?" and she just stood there and looked at me until I said "Music." The audiences must have thought we were crazy. Anyway, she finally gave in, and that night when I said, "What are you doing tonight?" she answered with, "I can't see you tonight, I'm expecting a headache." And it got a big laugh.

Back in the dressing room, I couldn't help gloating a little. I said to her, "Well, Gracie, haven't you got anything to say?"

She looked at me, smiled sweetly, and said, "George, pass the salt."

Now, from these last two stories don't get the wrong idea about Gracie. While she stood up for her rights and didn't want to be pushed around, she certainly had no desire to be a liberated woman. She enjoyed all the little niceties that were normally extended to women. She expected a man to

70

take off his hat in an elevator, pull out her chair for her when she sat down, and open a car door for her. Gracie behaved like a refined, gentle lady and felt she should be treated like one. Except for one night.

We were coming out of Toots Shor's restaurant in New York after dinner, and without thinking I walked out ahead of Gracie and forgot to hold the door open for her. I stood there on the sidewalk looking for a cab, and the next thing I knew Gracie came right up behind me. She lifted her skirt, kicked me right in the area I had recently been sitting on, and said, "George, you're no gentleman!"

When the cab came up, believe me, I held the door open for Gracie. I wanted to make sure that she got in ahead of me.

You see, like I said, looking back and reminiscing can be fun. I know it's been fun for me, and I hope you enjoyed it, too. If I had to sum up this chapter in a few words, I'd say, Learn to laugh at your problems! When everything seems to be going wrong, there's only one thing to do—just pass the salt! If there isn't any salt, pass the pepper, it works just as well!

Good Fathers Don't Grow on Trees

At times being my age can be embarrassing. People are always asking me for advice. I guess they figure if I've been around this long, I must know everything. Actually, I know very little, but sometimes you get backed into a corner. Like the other day at the club, Archie Preissman, a very successful businessman, came up to me and said, "George, do you think changing over to the metric system will have an effect on our economy?"

Well, I puffed my cigar, thought for a minute, did my impression of Bernard Baruch, and said, "That's funny, Archie, but Judge Roth just asked me the same thing. What do you think?"

"I think it will have a drastic effect on the economy," Archie answered.

I said, "That's exactly what I told Judge Roth."

"Thank you, George," Archie said, and walked away.

That's the way I am. When people ask me an opinion, I give it to them. Imagine asking me a question like that. I thought the metric system was a way to beat the horses.

Another time one of the members came up to me and said, "George, I'm really worried about my two teen-age sons. They stay out half the night, they drive too fast, they let their hair grow long, they dress like bums—what do you think I should do?"

Again I puffed on my cigar, thought for a minute, then did my impression of Dr. Spock and said, "Patience—you've got to have patience. By the time those kids get to be my age, believe me, you won't have to worry about them." He didn't even say thank you, he just walked away.

Now I don't claim to be an authority on parenthood, but Gracie and I did have two lovely children, Sandra (Sandy) and Ronnie. They're grown up now. Sandy has four beautiful daughters, Lori, Lissa, Grace-Anne, and Brooke (naturally, I'm teaching them harmony in case vaudeville comes back), and Ronnie has three handsome boys, Brent, Brad, and Bryan (with names like that they gotta wind up doing a dancing act). My grandchildren love to come over to visit me. They often come over on Friday and leave on Sunday. They look forward to these visits because I'm such a sweet, kind, considerate, lovable granddaddy. . . which is not true. The real reason they like to visit me is because of the two fine people working for me, Daniel and Arlette, who spend all their time entertaining the kids—that's the reason.

The kids don't even know I'm around. One day they were in swimming, and I was sitting by the pool. I overheard Brad say to Brent, "Who's the old man with the cigar?"

Brent looked over at me and said, "I'm not sure, but I think he's supposed to be our granddaddy."

When Gracie and I were raising Sandy and Ronnie, we were always in show business, so we had different problems than the average family. Our work hours were so irregular; sometimes we'd rehearse late, sometimes we had a very early call, sometimes we were on the road—so our problem was finding time to spend with the children. Most of the time we were able to have dinner with them. And, of course, we saw them on weekends. I don't know if Gracie and I were good parents or not, but we must have done something right, because Sandy and Ronnie turned out be a daughter and son I'm very proud of.

Naturally we had to discipline them from time to time. Once, when Sandy was five and Ronnie was four, we had a very expensive dictionary that we kept on a stand in the li-

My Grandchildren

Lori. *Photo by Jack Laxer.*

Lissa. *Photo by Jack Laxer.*

Left to right: Brad, Bryan, and Brent.

Grace-Anne.

Brooke.

brary. The dictionary was illustrated with beautiful colored pictures, and was actually a collector's item. When Gracie and I came home from the studio, we found the dictionary open and several of the pictures cut out of it. Well, Gracie was terribly upset and wanted to give the kids a good spanking. But I stopped her with, "Gracie, let me handle this. I'll use psychology and find out which one of them did it."

I called Ronnie into the room and said, "Ronnie, where did Sandy hide the scissors she used to cut out those pictures?"

Ronnie looked up at me and said, "I don't know, Daddy."

So I dismissed him and called in Sandy. "Sandy," I said, "where did Ronnie hide the scissors he used to cut out those pictures?"

"In that desk drawer, Daddy," she said, pointing.

Well, I looked in the drawer, and sure enough there were the scissors, and the case was solved. At that moment I thought to myself, I'm wasting my time in show business, I should be with the FBI. I went to Gracie and told her Ronnie was the one who cut out the pictures.

She said, "Well, we've got to teach him a lesson," and she called Ronnie into the room. She sat him down in a chair and said, "Ronnie, how do you spell chrysanthemum?"

Ronnie's eyes started to puddle up, and he said, "I don't know, Mommy."

Gracie said, "And you never will know if you go around cutting up dictionaries instead of reading them!"

After Ronnie had gone to his room, I said to Gracie, "How *do* you spell chrysanthemum?"

She gave me a look and said, "R-o-s-e, that's a flower, too!"

Anyway, solving that case sort of went to my head, so for years whenever anybody came to the house they had to listen to the story of how I solved the great dictionary caper. One night we were all gathered with friends in the living room, and I started to tell that story again. Sandy was now ten years old, and she stopped me. "Daddy," she said, "please don't tell that story anymore. You got it all wrong, anyway. It wasn't Ronnie. I knew the scissors were in that drawer because I was the one who cut out the pictures."

Well, that's when I resigned from the FBI and went back into show business.

When it came to entertaining the kids, again I had a problem. I knew that the average father was supposed to take his kids to the beach, go camping with them, take them fishing, hiking, go on picnics—but I just didn't have time for all those things. I'm sure Ronnie would have liked me to play baseball with him, but I knew nothing about baseball. I never played baseball. I played Mechanicsville, Schenectady, Scranton, Gloversville, Bristol, New Haven, Wilkes-Barre, Akron—but I was never booked in baseball.

I tried to entertain my kids in my own way, but I don't think they understood. I remember when they were still small and I was driving them home one night along Sunset Boulevard. They were repairing the street and they had put out about fifty of those warning lights that flash on and off. I stopped the car and said, "Look, kids, it's somebody's birthday! Now all together, let's sing!" and I started singing, "Happy Birthday to you . . . Happy Birthday to you . . . Happy Birthday, Sunset Boulevard, Happy Birthday to you. . . ." The kids looked at each other and joined in, but they didn't sing too loudly. All the rest of the way home neither one of them said a word. But as soon as we got to the house they rushed inside and went right to Gracie.

"Mommy," Sandy said, "I think something's wrong with Daddy. He saw a whole bunch of lights on the street and he thought it was a birthday cake."

Gracie kissed the children reassuringly and said, "Don't tell him it wasn't a birthday cake, it would spoil his fun."

Another time I really went to a lot of trouble to surprise Sandy and Ronnie. It was around Christmastime and Gracie and I were making a movie. On Christmas Eve I stayed late at the studio and had the wardrobe department fit me out with a whole Santa Claus outfit—the works; black leather boots, padded stomach, tasseled hat, and a big bag of toys. Then I went to the makeup department and they fixed me up with a big red nose, white bushy eyebrows, and they even glued on the white beard. When they got through with me I didn't even recognize myself.

I had let Gracie in on what I was planning, so when the doorbell rang at home that night, Gracie said, "Children, see who's at the door."

The kids opened the door, looked at me, and Ronnie said, "Mommy, Daddy's home."

When I walked in Gracie said to me, "George, your outfit is beautiful, but you should have left your cigar outside."

Here's another brainstorm I dreamed up to amuse the children. Sometimes I'd pick them up after kindergarten, and this one day when I was driving home I thought it would be funny if I drove up the wrong driveway—so I did. The kids started to jump up and down excitedly, and hollered, "Daddy, Daddy, you're in the wrong driveway, we don't live here!" I acted surprised and said, "Oh?" Then I backed out and drove home.

The next time I did it again, and this time I pulled into another driveway. Again the kids got excited and hollered, "Daddy, you're in the wrong driveway again!" I looked surprised and said "Oh?" Then I backed out and went home again.

The third time I did it I pulled into this driveway and drove clear back to the people's garage, but the kids just sat there and never said a word. I stopped the car and said, "Aren't you going to tell me I'm in the wrong driveway?"

Sandy said, "No. Mommy said we should let you enjoy yourself."

That was the end of that hilarious bit.

The years flew by, the kids grew older, and so did my sense of humor. When Ronnie was about fifteen he came to me one day right at the beginning of summer vacation, full of enthusiasm, and asked me if he could build a boat in the backyard. I was all for it; I thought it was a great idea and even offered to pay for the lumber. I figured it would be worth it; building a boat would keep him occupied, teach him how to work with his hands, and he wouldn't be running around getting into trouble all summer. I was sure a project like that would take three months, but four days later Ronnie came to me and said, "Dad, the boat's finished."

I went out in the backyard and, sure enough, there was this little boat, about five feet long. I said, "Ronnie, you did a nice job, but that boat is barely big enough to hold you. I thought you were going to build a boat—a real boat—something that you and your friends could get on and sail to Catalina."

"But, Dad," Ronnie said, "that would take my whole summer vacation."

I said, "Supposing it does. That little thing you built wouldn't even get you across the swimming pool." I paused a moment, then continued with, "But wouldn't it be great when you go back to school if you could say to the other kids, 'I just finished building a boat that could take us all to Catalina'?"

I waited while Ronnie gave this some deep thought. Finally he said enthusiastically, "Dad, I'll do it. I'll get some of my pals to help me and we'll start real early at seven o'clock in the morning."

"Ronnie," I said, "you better make it eight thirty. Beverly Hills is not zoned for a shipyard."

That night I confided to Gracie, "We don't have to worry about Ronnie this summer. He'll be out in the backyard building another *Queen Mary*."

Well, the weeks went by and the boat got bigger and bigger, and so did Ronnie's labor crew. Every day there were about fifteen kids out there hammering and sawing and yelling. The swimming pool was full of shavings and sawdust, there was so much lumber stacked up we could hardly get out the back door, and every day at lunchtime we had to feed that bunch. And when it comes to food, a fifteen-year-old kid is like a human disposal. I won't say how much I spent on food, but that summer the little market where we bought our groceries became the Safeway chain.

Finally, at the end of summer, Ronnie came running in and said, "Dad, we finished the boat—but we got a problem." Boy, did we have a problem! The only way we could have gotten that boat out of the backyard would have been to tear down the house. Well, Ronnie went back to school with a hand covered with blisters, and I had to hire carpenters to come and dismantle the boat. And as the last load of lumber went down the driveway, Gracie said to me, "George, next summer try to think of something to keep Ronnie out of the backyard."

I didn't have to, Ronnie thought of something himself. During that school year Ronnie's grades were not the greatest, so at the end of the term I felt he should go to summer school. But by this time Ronnie had discovered surfing. Every daylight hour he and Freddie Astaire, Jr., were at the beach. I knew I had to do something, so I said to him, "Ronnie, you've been bugging me to buy you a car, so I'll make a deal with you. If you go to summer school, you've got the car."

Ronnie said, "Dad, it's a deal."

So I bought him a nice little car and figured that problem was solved—but it wasn't. Ronnie started getting up at five o'clock in the morning, then he'd drive to the beach and surf for a couple of hours, then drive to summer school, go to his first class, and promptly fall asleep. It took me a couple of weeks to find out I'd been had. But there was nothing I could do about it. The deal was that if I bought Ronnie a car, he'd go to summer school—and that he was doing. There was no clause in the deal that said he couldn't sleep through the classes.

This new problem might have defeated a lesser man, but not me. I came right back with what I thought was a stroke of psychological genius. The next morning at four o'clock I went into Ronnie's room, shook him awake, and sat on the edge of the bed. Remembering how Lewis Stone talked to

Mickey Rooney in the "Andy Hardy" series, I said, "Ronnie, since you don't seem to be much interested in school, you should start giving some serious thought to your future. Now, you and Freddie go to Malibu Beach every morning, and that beach is known all over the world; the sand there has got to be very valuable. If you and Freddie took that sand and canned it, you kids could sell it and make a fortune."

Ronnie looked at me like I had a hole in my head, took the covers, and pulled them over his face. Well, at five o'clock Ronnie got up, drove to the beach, did his surfing, drove to school, fell asleep—and at four o'clock the next morning I was shaking him awake again. "Ronnie," I said, "wake up. You and Freddie better get down to that beach and start canning that sand. Some other kids might steal the idea and there'll be no sand left. You and Freddie could lose a fortune." Ronnie never said a word, he just got up and went into the bathroom and locked the door.

Well, this went on for four days. Finally Ronnie came to me and said, "Okay, Dad, you win. Freddie and I have given up surfing."

I was glad to hear this because I was getting pretty tired of getting up at four o'clock every morning.

"We've now taken up scuba diving," Ronnie continued.

"Scuba diving!" I said.

He said, "Yeah, that idea of yours about canning the sand was so good we decided to branch out. Freddie and I are going to start bottling genuine Malibu salt water, too. So long, Dad." And he left.

Well, Andy Hardy had beaten Lewis Stone at his own game.

The value of my parenthood extended beyond Ronnie, however. There was my daughter Sandy, who was a beautiful girl. When she was sixteen she was going steady with a fellow named Red something-or-other, I forget his name. Anyway, Red was a football player and about six feet, five inches tall. He was so solid and had such bulging muscles

81

he didn't look like he was born; he looked like he was put together with an erector set.

Every day Sandy and Red would come home after school and sit on the floor in the library and watch television. I had never met Red until one day when I came into the library from the club, and there he was. Even sitting on the floor he was taller than I was. Anyway, they both got up, Sandy introduced me, and when Red shook hands with me he broke all my fingers. Well, he didn't really break them, but the next day when I played bridge somebody else had to hold my cards for me.

The next time I met Red the same thing happened again. This time he squeezed my hand so hard it blew out the crystal of my wristwatch. I knew I had to do something.

A couple of days later, when I came home, there stood Red with his hand out. I quickly put both of my hands in my pockets and said, "Hold it, Red. You're a nice young boy, but you don't know your own strength. From now on when we meet we don't have to shake hands. You just say 'Hello, Mr. Burns,' and I'll say 'Hello, Red.' "

He grinned and said, "I guess I am pretty strong, and I'll never do it again. Let's shake on it, Mr. Burns," and he reached into my pocket, grabbed my hand, and there went my fingers again. I was very happy when Sandy dumped Red and started going round with a small flute player in the school band.

To sum it up, it's a good thing I didn't have to make a living being a father. I would have ended up on welfare. But now that I'm older I'm much wiser, and when people come to me for advice I'm able to help them. If you don't believe me, read the beginning of this chapter again where I helped Archie Preissman and Judge Roth with the metric system.

A Newcomer at Sixty-two

Sometimes almost all of us reach a point in our life at which it becomes necessary to make a change. If this happens when you're young, it's easy, but when you have to make a change in your later years it may not be easy, but nevertheless you've still got to make it.

On June 4, 1958, the last episode of the Burns & Allen show was filmed, and Gracie retired. I didn't blame her. She had spent all her life worrying about wardrobe, makeup, getting her hair done, and rehearsals. And, after we got into television, learning thirty to forty pages of dialogue every week. Gracie wanted to relax and be able to spend some time with our grandchildren.

But I wasn't ready to retire. I was only sixty-two years old and fresh as a daisy. After all, I'd been retired all those years I was on the stage with Gracie.

Well, I came up with an idea that I thought was absolutely brilliant. Through the years of Burns & Allen we developed sort of a stock company of very talented people; like Bea Benadaret, Larry Keating, Harry Von Zell, and my son Ronnie. So why not surround myself with those same people and call it *The George Burns Show*? It seemed like a natural. I was so enthused that my writers and I knocked out a script and sold it to the Colgate people without even making a pilot. They bought it for twenty-six weeks. They made a mistake. So did I, and it was a beauty. It didn't take a genius to figure out what was wrong. Sure, we had the same people, but any minute you expected Gracie to come through the door. It was like having dinner; we had the soup, the salad, and the dessert, but the main course was home playing with her grandchildren.

At the end of the twenty-six weeks the show went off the air, and there I was at the bottom again. I knew that sooner or later I'd bounce back, but I had to figure out how. I'd never worked alone before, so I had to find an image for myself. People like Jack Benny, Bob Hope, Milton Berle, all the established comedians, had spent years developing their characters, but here I was, a kid of sixty-two, struggling to get into show business.

Well, again I came up with an idea I thought was absolutely brilliant. As long as I needed an identity, why not be me? That took me right to the bottom again, because I said to myself, "Who's me?" Sure, I was funny at parties—I sang old patter songs that everybody laughed at—I told amusing anecdotes—and I was usually the hit of the sociable. . . . I thought that over for a while, and all of a sudden I said, "Wait a minute—that's me!" And it was.

I sat down with my writers and we put together a nightclub act in which I did exactly what I'd been doing at parties. I opened with a monologue of amusing anecdotes, I sang some of my old patter songs, and I booked myself into Bill Harrah's club at Lake Tahoe. But I wasn't taking any chances; I brought along Bobby Darin, who was sensational, the DeCastro Sisters, who sang up a storm, and one of the great dancing acts, Brascia & Tybee.

My opening night at Harrah's was practically one year to the day after Gracie retired. When I walked out on that stage for the first time in my life alone, believe me, it was a strange feeling. Anyway, I took a deep breath, lit my cigar, and said:

> Ladies and gentlemen, this is the first time I ever played a nightclub, and I hate people who come out and say they're nervous. I despise myself, but I am.
> All my friends had advice for me. I ran into Dean Martin,

and he told me to relax like he does. I tried it, but it gave me the hiccups.

And Frank Sinatra said, "George, there's nothing to be nervous about. When you get to Harrah's, just do what I do." At my age that's even harder than drinking.

Everybody wanted to help. Sammy Davis offered to lend me his uncle.

Sophie Tucker said, "George, I've played cafés all my life. I'm seventy-two years old, and now my voice is gone, it's practically shot, and I'm still a big hit. So you can't miss. You've got what it took me seventy-two years to get."

Even Zsa Zsa Gabor called me. She said, "George, you've got to be a hit at Harrah's if you do what I do." Not me. If I listened to her and Sinatra, I couldn't last half an hour. And if I took the advice of Frank Sinatra, Dean Martin and Sammy Davis, I'd be worn out . . . have a hangover . . . and an uncle who doesn't look like me.

And my close friend, Jack Benny, gave me some advice, too.

(Pointing)

He's sitting right down there. Before the show tonight he came backstage and said, "George, I've been working alone for a lot of years and I'll give you a little tip that's helped me. If you do this, you can't miss. After each joke you tell, just look at the audience, and keep looking, because if you look long enough, they must laugh."

"Jack," I said, "what happens if I look at the audience and they look back at me longer than I look at them?"

He said, "George, that's your problem—I'll be sitting out front."

(to Jack)

Jack, I love you.

(to audience)

And Jack is such a sport. Last night when we arrived he went to the dice table, and they're still talking about it. He held the dice for forty-five minutes. He finally threw them and rolled a crap. He lost five dollars and they had to hold *him* for forty-five minutes.

But the reason my friends are all trying to help me is that basically I'm not a comedian. I'm a straight man. You know what a straight man is—he just repeats things. The comedian or comedienne asks a question, he repeats the question, and they get a laugh. I've been a straight man for so long I went fishing with a fellow once, he fell overboard and hollered "Help!" I repeated "Help!", and while I was waiting for him to get his laugh, he drowned. He must have thought he was funny, because he came up, took three bows, and disappeared.

But you know, it's awfully strange for me to be out here on the stage alone, because after all, I worked with Gracie for thirty-eight years. But now she's retired. And believe me, when Gracie retired she didn't fool around, she really retired. She's even thinking of getting twin beds.

I married Gracie in Cleveland a long time ago. And after the ceremony Gracie looked up at me and said, "I always knew a handsome man would marry me." She was right—that justice of the peace was the best-looking fellow you ever saw. Not to disappoint Gracie, I asked him to come along on our honeymoon.

But I love it here at Lake Tahoe. However, everybody is so nice to you, you can't get a good night's sleep. The owner of this place, Bill Harrah, is quite a host. At three o'clock this morning he sent up a complimentary cocktail. So what could I do? The waiter helped me out of bed, I poured it into my hot milk, and I drank it.

At five thirty the maid came in and gave me some fresh towels. I haven't had to use a fresh towel at five thirty in the morning, June the twentieth will be thirty-seven years.

Ten minutes later the honeymoon couple next door started arguing about their wedding—they couldn't decide where to have it.

And when I finally did get to sleep I had a horrible dream. I dreamed I was alone on a desert island with Ava Gardner and Lana Turner. I suppose you're wondering what would make a dream like that so horrible. In it I was Rita Hayworth.

Anyway, there we were, just three girls on this island. . . . Who do you think was washed ashore? Lawrence Welk. Whom do you think he went for? Me. . . . All night long, a-one and a-two . . .

86

But don't worry, even though I didn't get a good night's sleep it hasn't affected my singing voice. I love to sing. I can't help it, there's something deep inside of me that just has to come out. If you had something like that inside of you, you'd want it out, too.

Now, I know you all came here to listen to some great singing, and I'm not going to disappoint you . . .

Ladies and gentlemen—Bobby Darin!

Well, Bobby Darin was a smash and so were the DeCastro Sisters and Brascia & Tybee. The whole show was great. After the opening everybody came backstage and congratulated me. But later that night when Gracie and I were alone, I said, "Gracie, how did you like me tonight?"

She said, "I thought it was a wonderful show."

"Gracie, what did you think of me?"

"George, you surrounded yourself with marvelous people."

Right then I knew she was holding something back. I said, "Come on, Gracie, let's have it."

"Well," she said, "your songs were just fine, but when you went into your monologues you knew them too well. You sounded like you were reciting them."

I was stunned! My first reaction was to be resentful, but before I could even say anything she added, "George, I know that what I just said upset you, but I think all you have to do is be natural. Like when you're entertaining at parties everybody loves you because you're just being yourself."

That's all that was said, but I didn't sleep that night. All night long I lay there wide awake, practicing how to be natural. It took quite a while, but I finally licked it. I got to the point where I could walk out on the stage and act like I was at a party, and I've been having parties with audiences ever since.

Onstage Gracie played the part of a kooky dame, but offstage I learned to listen to her because that girl knew what she was talking about.

Anyway, there I was, sixty-two years old and starting a brand-new career. It was a wonderful feeling. I found that audiences enjoyed my songs and laughed at my monologues. In fact, I got so darned good I invested in a new eyebrow pencil.

A Dresser Is not a Piece of Furniture

I don't know if this is common knowledge or not, but most performers in show business who are doing well have what is known as a dresser. In this case a dresser is not a piece of furniture, he's someone whose main function is to take care of your clothes and help you in and out of them. But it goes a lot further than that, especially if you're traveling. He's your road manager . . . your secretary . . . if you want a sandwich in your dressing room he gets it for you . . . he sees that your suits are pressed and your shoes shined . . . he picks up your airplane tickets and makes sure that your luggage is taken care of . . . in fact, he does everything possible to make you comfortable so you're free to concentrate on giving a good performance. That's a dresser, and believe me, it's a full-time job.

Now in all the years that Gracie and I traveled together we never thought of having a dresser. Gracie took care of her own clothes, I used to zip her up, and nobody had to help me. I always knew how to put my pants on: First you put in one leg, then you put in the other—I learned that when I was fourteen years old. My mother was so proud of me. I got so good at it she used to call in the neighbors to watch me do it.

But then, in 1958, when Gracie retired and I started working alone, I had to travel a lot, so I hired a dresser. Not that I needed one, but after all those years of working with Gracie I couldn't get used to being in a dressing room by myself. I needed company, somebody to kick gags around with.

I hired this dresser when I got booked into Las Vegas, and he was a beautiful-looking man who came highly recommended. But he was so perfect he drove me right up the wall. Everything was, "Yes, Mr. Burns"; "No, Mr. Burns"; "I'll get it for you, Mr. Burns"; "I've got it for you, Mr. Burns"; "I'll tie it for you, Mr. Burns"; "I'll untie it for you, Mr. Burns"—he wouldn't let me do anything for myself. Then one day, when he tried to help me put my socks on, that was the end. I learned to do that when I was fifteen.

After I let him go, there I was, lonesome again. One morning I was sitting in the coffee shop all by myself having breakfast when I heard a voice say, "Hi, George!" I looked up, and standing there was Charlie Reade. I hadn't seen Charlie since he was part of one of the most famous dancing acts in vaudeville, called The Dunhills. The act is still around, but with different people. Charlie was one of the original Dunhills. I was very glad to see him and invited him to sit down and have some breakfast. We got to talking about old times, and it turned out that Charlie had split up with his partners years ago and had wound up in Las Vegas looking for something to do, but so far nothing had turned up.

So I got an idea. I said, "Charlie, how would you like to work for me?"

He said, "Doing what?"

"Be my dresser."

Charlie stopped with a bite of egg halfway to his mouth. Then he put the fork down on the plate and slowly pushed the plate away. After a swallow of water he wiped his lips with the napkin, placed the napkin on the table, and then, deliberately folding his arms, he looked me right in the eye. There was a pause of about five seconds, and then he said, "George, would you mind repeating that?"

Well Charlie had given such a great performance, and not wanting to be outdone, I decided to give one, too. I dramatically put down my fork, slowly pushed my plate away, took a swallow of water, wiped my lips with the napkin, deliberately folded my arms, and stared right back at him. "How would you like to be my dresser?" I repeated.

Still looking right at me, Charlie said, "A dresser?! George, I'm a *dancer!*"

"All right, Charlie," I said, "before you say no, the job pays two-hundred and fifty dollars a week and all your expenses."

I sat there waiting for an answer. Finally Charlie said, "George, I'll take the job under one condition—promise that you won't tell anybody that I'm your dresser."

I said, "Charlie, you've got a deal. I'll tell everybody you're my road manager."

He said, "Great," and finished his breakfast. And since he was now on an expense account he ordered strawberry shortcake for dessert.

That was the beginning of a long and interesting relationship with Charlie Reade. He moved in with me and we were together practically twenty-four hours a day. He was marvelous company, and we had a lot of laughs because we both spoke the same language.

Charlie was really a beautiful dancer. He was considered to be one of the best. In fact, he was one of the few dancers who could do what is called a heel roll. He'd put his weight on the ball of his foot and tap so fast with his heel that it sounded like a machine gun. There wasn't any style of dancing that Charlie couldn't do, and his idol was Fred Astaire. Charlie dressed like Astaire, he moved like Astaire, he even walked like him. When I went down the street with him I felt like Ginger Rogers.

With Charlie everything was dancing, and me being an old hoofer, I went right along with it. We always had twin beds in our hotel room, and sometimes before we went to sleep we'd play a little game. Charlie would move his feet under the covers, and by watching the movement I'd try to guess which step he was doing. I'd say, "I've got it, Charlie, you're doing *Falling off a Log.*" He'd say, "Right, George, now it's your turn." Then he'd watch my feet under the covers and say, "George, you're doing *Off to Buffalo,*" and I'd say, "You're wrong, I'm doing *Over the Top.*" If anybody had walked in on us we would have wound up on the funny farm.

Charlie even talked tap dancing, and I understood him. I recall one night when I was playing at the Sahara Hotel and we were having dinner between shows. Charlie was explaining a dance routine he put together. He said, "It goes like this, George. You start with a time step and then go into—

>Boppa doppa, boppa doppa, boppa doppa dop
>Babop, babop, babop, babop, babop, babop
>Doodlely-doo bop bop, doodlely-doo bop bop
>Doodlely-doo, doodlely-doo, doodlely-doo bop!"

Right in the middle of Charlie's routine, while I was nodding my head in tempo, a man tapped me on the shoulder. He said, "Mr. Burns, I enjoyed your show very much, but I'd like to ask you something. I was sitting at the next table, and I speak seven foreign languages—but what language is your friend speaking?"

I said, "I haven't the faintest idea, but I understand him perfectly."

The man just shook his head and walked away.

Following Vegas I was booked into Harrah's Club at Lake Tahoe. By now I had found out that my new dresser (I mean road manager) had several peculiar little quirks. Like when he took my shoes down to the barbershop to be shined, he would always carry them in a flight bag so that nobody would know that was one of his duties. One day I was in the barbershop getting a haircut, and the barber said, "Mr. Burns, what's wrong with that road manager of yours? Every day around one o'clock he comes in with a pair of shoes in a flight bag and whispers to my shoeshine boy, "I'll pick these up in an hour and don't take them out of the bag until I leave the shop,' and then he ducks out."

I said, "Well, I'm surprised he brings both of them in at the same time. He's very particular about his shoes. He usually brings in one first, and if he likes the shine, he brings in the other one. He must really trust that kid you got working for you."

The barber never said a word, all I could hear was the snipping of his scissors. But on my way out I couldn't resist taking a parting shot. I said to the barber, "If I were you, I'd give that shoeshine kid a raise. You got a gold mine there."

Besides smuggling my shoes in and out, another one of Charlie's duties was to help me on with my coat when I got dressed for a performance. But Charlie had so much pride that he always made sure the dressing room door was closed so nobody would see him holding my coat. One night the owner of the hotel, Bill Harrah, walked in while Charlie was holding my coat, and without missing a beat Charlie put it on and pretended it was his. Well, so as not to embarrass Charlie I put on his coat. Both of us looked pretty silly; him in checkered pants and a tuxedo coat, and me in a checkered coat and tuxedo pants. Bill Harrah stared at us and said, "I don't want to say anything, but you fellows have your coats mixed up."

Looking down, I said, "I didn't notice that," and so Charlie and I changed coats.

Charlie traveled with me for six years, and he was a delight to be with. He was cheerful and had a great sense of humor, and we spent hours talking together because both of us knew nothing but show business. It was never dull being with Charlie because you never knew what he'd come up with next. I was getting dressed one evening and I noticed that Charlie was standing in the hall outside the dressing room and leaning against the door frame. I said, "Charlie, why are you standing out there? Come on in."

He said, "No, George, this parquet floor out here has a nice feel to it."

Now, nobody else would have understood that, but right away I knew exactly what he meant. It was a dancer's floor.

93

So I went out there and stood with him, and Charlie was right, it was the nicest floor I ever stood on.

Another one of Charlie's duties was to go down with me and stand in the wings just before I went out on the stage. In one hand he carried a glass of scotch and water, and in the other a glass of sand. Just before my entrance I always took a healthy slug of scotch, and after my monologue I'd come offstage and pour some of the sand in my pocket. I used the sand to sprinkle on the floor for my sand dance. Well, one night just as my entrance music started, I said, "Charlie, give me the scotch." Charlie handed me the wrong glass, and I took a healthy slug of sand. Did you ever try to say, "Good evening, ladies and gentlemen," with a mouthful of sand? I don't know how I got through that performance, but in the middle of it I glanced into the wings and there was Charlie drinking my scotch and water. From that night on, Charlie's backstage duties were cut in half; he carried the glass of sand and I carried my own scotch.

I don't think I mentioned this, but this might be a good time to do so. From time to time Charlie would do a little nipping, and sometimes he'd overdo it. When this happened Charlie would get a little temperamental. In fact, he had a pretty good-sized temper. One night in Vegas we were in a taxicab on our way to see a lounge show and we got into some kind of silly argument. I don't even remember what it was about, but all of a sudden in an angry voice Charlie said to the cabdriver, "Pull over to the curb!" The cab stopped and Charlie opened the door. Without even glancing at me he said, "George, I've had enough of you! Get out!"

I very quietly said, "Charlie, you're a little mixed up. I'm not working for you, you're working for me."

"Oh?" he said. "Then I'll get out!" Which he did.

I went on to see the lounge show, and five minutes later in walked Charlie and sat down at my table. I said, "Charlie, how about a cup of black coffee?"

He said, "Good idea." Then he added, "Tell the waiter to put a little rum in it."

Then there was the time when Charlie just disappeared without a word. For two days I called every hotel in town, checked all the places he hung out, but there was no sign of him. I was really getting worried when on the third day Charlie showed up out of the blue. I waited for an explanation, but he acted like nothing had happened. When I couldn't stand it any longer, I said, "Charlie, where the hell have you been?"

He said, "George, I had to get away for a couple of days. You're a strong personality, and being around you all the time I was losing my identity."

Trying to make light of it, I said, "Well, Charlie, I'll try to stop smiling so much."

He said, "No, George, I'm serious. I had to be alone to see if I could find myself."

I knew he meant it, so I said, "Charlie, I hope it worked."

"I think it did," he nodded.

"Good," I said, and for the rest of the week I held my own coat.

I wouldn't say that Charlie was a particularly religious man, but every once in a while he'd go to mass. One Sunday morning, after he'd been to an early mass, we were having breakfast together. I was playing Reno that week, and I said, "Charlie, I rented a car, so after breakfast why don't we take a little drive?"

He had been very quiet all through breakfast, and when I suggested the drive, he said, "No, George, this is Sunday. I'm going to walk up into the hills, and when I get to the top I might run into Him."

I didn't want to discourage him, so I said, "Okay, Charlie, but if you do run into Him, I'm afraid you might be disappointed, He doesn't dance. And if He did, He'd be pretty awkward wearing those sandals."

Charlie gave me a look and, getting up from the table, said, "George, for a comedian you're not very funny." And then he left.

I sat there and watched through the windows as he

walked off toward the foothills. Only Charlie Reade would go looking for Jesus in Reno.

When Charlie came to work for me he was no kid. I'd say he was about fifty years old. But he was in great physical shape because he never stopped dancing. He had a trim waistline, he was very light on his feet, and he took great pride in his sense of balance. But there was one time when Charlie's balance deserted him. It was up at Lake Tahoe, and after one of our midnight shows I went to bed and Charlie went out on the town. I don't know whether it was the altitude or a few too many belts of booze, but around three o'clock in the morning I got a phone call from the manager of the Hi-Ho Bar and Grill. "Mr. Burns, does a fellow named Charlie Reade live with you?" he said.

"That's right," I answered.

"Well, he just fell off a barstool and hurt himself."

"Is it anything serious?" I asked.

The voice on the phone said, "No, he just got a cut on the back of his head. What should I do?"

I said, "Either take him to a hospital or have him wear his hat."

Well, after I hung up I got to thinking that maybe I should go down there and see if Charlie was okay. So I got dressed, jumped in a cab, and rushed down to the Hi-Ho Bar and Grill. When I walked in, the juke box was playing and there was Charlie with his hat on, doing one of his dance routines.

Charlie and I are still friends, and I hear from him all the time. Believe me, if I ever go on the road again, Charlie Reade will not only be my road manager, but I might even hire a dresser for him.

Here She Is, Ladies and Gentlemen— Mrs. Charles Lowe!

You know, when I started appearing in nightclubs it was quite a change for me. After working practically all my life with Gracie, here I found myself working with new people every season. And they were all very talented people. Then, in 1962, I was lucky enough to team up with a tall, wide-eyed, open-faced blonde with a wild, dizzy, cockeyed sense of humor. From that description I'm sure you know whom I mean—Mrs. Charles Lowe. Some of her intimate friends know her better as Carol Channing.

I knew Charlie and Carol before they were married. Charlie was working with the Burns & Allen television show as a sponsor representative. He got started in the business as a public relations man for Aimee Semple MacPherson (I'm not sure, but I think Charlie was the one who introduced her to Milton Berle). I met Carol through Charlie, and as soon as I met her there was an immediate feeling of mutual admiration. Carol and Charlie, and Gracie and I, became very close friends, and it seemed inevitable that Carol and I would wind up working together.

And we did! We put a show together with four other acts and called it the *George Burns-Carol Channing Show*. Everybody thought that was a very clever title for a show. In all modesty, I must say I thought of it myself.

Our first booking was at the Orpheum theater in Seattle during the Seattle World's Fair. It was a very good show, and we did very good business. We had sort of a vaudeville format, and at the end of the show Carol and I did a Burns &

Allen routine and then finished with a song and a sand dance.

I had never done a comedy routine like that with anybody but Gracie, but with Carol's off-beat personality I thought the routine we did would be a natural. But something was wrong. We were getting laughs, but there was something missing; there was no relationship . . . we weren't a team. After the third performance I finally figured out what the trouble was. When I worked with Gracie, she spoke directly to me; she looked at me and I looked at her. To Gracie there were no footlights—to her that was a wall and she never knew there was an audience out there. Now, Carol was the exact opposite. She played everything directly to the audience and didn't know I was out there.

Well, once I knew what the problem was I solved it. The next performance, when we came out on the stage, Carol didn't look at me—I didn't look at her—and we both worked straight to the audience. Now that I was working the same way as Carol, it felt right—we were finally a team. Do you know that Carol never even knew I changed my style! She was so in love with that audience she didn't know what I was doing out there anyway.

This is the way we played the routine. And remember—we both said everything directly to the audience:

Carol and George enter from opposite sides and meet center stage.

GEORGE
Ladies and gentlemen, Carol is now going to say hello to everybody.

CAROL
Hello, everybody.

GEORGE
Let's see, how should we start?

CAROL
I always like to start with a joke.

98

GEORGE
I think Carol's got a good idea there.

CAROL
All right. I took my girlfriend to the doctor's today, and while I was there somebody told this joke that had everybody dying laughing.

GEORGE
I'm sure we'd all like to hear it.

CAROL
Well, it went like this: "Don't let that upset you, he never says good-bye to anybody!" (A long pause)

GEORGE
That can't be the whole joke.

CAROL
There was some stuff ahead of it that I didn't hear, but that was the line that had everybody dying laughing.

GEORGE
I think we better find another way to start.

CAROL
This might be interesting. While I was in the doctor's office I read a newspaper that had the latest census report on this city. And you people out there don't look tired and worn out.

GEORGE
Tired and worn out? You don't look that way to me, either.

CAROL
Well, right at the top of the census report it said, "Population of Seattle—broken down by age and sex!"

GEORGE
I don't think she understands what that means.

CAROL
Ohhhhh, yes I do. I've known about the birds and the bees all my life.

GEORGE
That's a surprise to me.

CAROL

When I was a little girl my mother told me how the bees carry pollen from flower to flower on their feet. I even tried it, and it's nothing.

GEORGE

I'm sorry to hear that—I was getting ready to take off my shoes.

CAROL

And I read something else in the newspaper while I was in the doctor's office. A very rich man died, and the lawyer read his will to his sons and daughters and their husbands and wives. It said for every new child that was born they would get an extra half million dollars, but they weren't interested.

GEORGE

That's hard to believe.

CAROL

Well, they weren't. Before he even finished reading the will the room was empty.

GEORGE

The reason they ran out was they were probably double-parked.

CAROL

Anyway, this doctor has a beautiful redheaded nurse with the most gorgeous figure. But she was sick, too, poor little thing. She kept begging the doctor to take her appendix out.

GEORGE

Can you folks imagine a beautiful nurse asking a doctor to take out her appendix?

CAROL

It's true. Every time she went into his private office I could hear her hollering, "Doctor, please, cut it out!"

GEORGE

That doctor really knew how to operate.

CAROL

Let me tell you folks why my girlfriend went to see the doctor in the first place. She went to have the dents taken out of her knees.

GEORGE

Well, if you've got dents in your knees, that's the place to go.

CAROL

That's what she had. When I looked in the office, the doctor was pounding them out with a little rubber hammer.

GEORGE

He was trying to get a look at her reflexes.

CAROL

Well, no wonder she kept kicking at him. . . . And while she was in the doctor's office I cheered up all the patients in the waiting room. There was one little boy there who looked so sad, so I took him around and made everyone shake hands with him. It made him so happy he almost forgot he had the measles.

GEORGE

Carol's friendliness is really contagious.

CAROL

I helped the nurse, too. I answered the phone for her. Somebody wanted to know if a man eighty-five years old could have rickets.

GEORGE

I can't wait to hear what her answer was.

CAROL

I said let him have all he wants as long as he chews them well.

GEORGE

For a minute I thought she might give the wrong answer, but she fooled me.

CAROL

And then the doctor from the next office came in, and he was whistling.

GEORGE

He must have had something to whistle about.

CAROL

The nurse said that he was Dr. Brown, the famous obstetrician. She said that last year he had two hundred and sixty babies.

GEORGE

Well, that's wonderful.

CAROL

It might be wonderful for him, but I'll bet his wife isn't whistling.

GEORGE

I'd like to straighten her out, but she's so happy the way she is.

CAROL

I tried to have a talk with that doctor, but he was in a hurry to get back to his office. He said he had a little boy in there a year and a half old who couldn't hold on to his food. So I said, "Why don't you give him a live lobster? If he can't hold on to his food, give him food that can hold on to him."

GEORGE

I'll bet that doctor wasn't whistling when he left.

CAROL

Then this woman sitting next to me told me she sprained her back playing tennis. She told me that she hadn't held a racket in her hand for two years. So I said, "My goodness, where have you been holding it?"

That was our music cue. We sang "Some of These Days," did a sand dance, and that was the finish of the show. This whole bit ran about eight minutes, and not once did we look at each other.

That was Carol Channing onstage. Let me tell you about her offstage—the real Carol Channing—the zany one.

Now, most people have more than one personality. And I'm not speaking about only show business people, I'm talking about everybody. Just think about it—if you're at a dinner party and you're sitting next to your wife, your person-

102

ality is entirely different than if you were sitting next to somebody else's wife—especially if she's pretty—especially if she's got her hand on your knee—especially if she whispers her phone number into your ear. You're oozing charm and personality until you glance across the table and see your wife glaring at you, wise to the whole thing. One minute you're Rudolph Valentino, Cary Grant, and Warren Beatty all rolled into one, and in that split second you're back to What's-His-Name again.

And if you're a woman, this whole personality thing works in reverse. Say you're at the same party and you're dancing with your husband. You're bored to tears, you're looking around to see what the other women are wearing, and your husband is telling you about his day at the office, but you're not even listening. In fact, you don't even know the music is playing. But ten minutes later and you're dancing with that handsome Dr. Jarvis. Your feet don't even touch the floor as he's holding you close, and you're moving even closer as you laugh at all his witty remarks. You're happy—you're gay—you're Miss Universe! You look around for your husband, positive he'll be in a jealous rage. But where is he? He's at the bar with that broad he was on the make for at the dinner table. That'll put a kink in your personality!

You'll notice I had the man come out on top in that story. Look, I believe in Women's Lib, but I still like to see a guy get lucky once in a while. What I'm trying to say is that everybody changes his or her personality to fit any given situation; that is, everybody but Carol Channing. Her personality is bigger than life. To her, everything is show business. If she goes to the bathroom, it's an exit—when she comes out, it's an entrance. When she and Charlie go to bed at night she's so full of show business that Charlie has to keep applauding her until she falls asleep. And in the morning if he doesn't give her a standing ovation, she won't get up!

Now, here's a story Charlie told me. I don't believe it, but here it is anyway. One night they were staying at the Waldorf in New York, and two robbers broke into their room. Carol woke up, and one of the burglars turned his flashlight on her. She went right into two choruses of "Diamonds Are a Girl's Best Friend." The burglars applauded and left. That's such a good lie I'm sorry I gave Charlie credit for it.

During the fourteen weeks Carol and I worked together there was never a dull moment. Working with Carol was exciting, and I enjoyed it. But like with any relationship from time to time there were problems. Like the night we opened in Seattle—the first half of the show was supposed to run an hour and twenty-five minutes; then a ten-minute intermission; and the second half was supposed to run forty-five minutes, which would bring the curtain down exactly at ten thirty.

Well, the first half went fine, but in the second half when Carol came on to do her thirty minutes she stayed there an hour and a half. That night the final curtain didn't come down until eleven thirty. This meant we had to pay the musicians and stagehands one hour of Golden Time, which ran into a lot of money.

I explained this to Carol, but she looked up at me with those great big wide eyes and said, "Why, George, I can't believe I was on stage for ninety minutes. In fact, I thought I was running short tonight; I almost added another number." Well, that's Carol. When she's out there she falls in love with the audience, and the audience falls in love with her, and time means nothing. She felt terrible about what had happened, and apologized and promised it would never happen again.

However, I wasn't taking any chances. The next night when Carol was in the middle of singing "I'm Just a Little Girl from Litte Rock," I walked out onstage, stopped the music, and pointed to my watch. Carol batted those big eyes at me, then turned to the audience and said, "Ladies and gentlemen, my thirty minutes are up!" and we went into our double routine.

With Carol you never know what's going to happen next.

She lives in a world all her own. We were playing the Dunes Hotel in Las Vegas, and during the eight weeks we were there I wanted to change some of the jokes. So one day I knocked on her dressing room and said, "Carol, are you decent?"

She called out, "Sure, but I'm not dressed. Come in."

So I went in, and there she was sitting at the makeup table with absolutely nothing on but a little towel over her lap. I just stood there; I didn't know what to do. So I kept looking at the ceiling—after all, her husband, Charlie, was a very close friend of mine.

Very matter-of-factly Carol said, "What do you want, George?"

I stammered a bit. "I—I—I—I'd like to change some jokes in the act."

"Just a second, George," Carol said. "I'll be with you as soon as I put my eyelashes on."

Well, I left, in a hurry. With Carol, when she puts her eyelashes on she thinks she's fully dressed.

In all the time I've known Carol I've never known her to miss a performance. But one day in Las Vegas I thought this was it. Around five thirty in the evening one time I was over at the Riviera Hotel having a drink with Tony Martin when they paged me over the loudspeaker in the bar. When I answered the call a very excited operator said, "Thank heavens I've found you, Mr. Burns! I've paged you in every hotel in Las Vegas!"

It sounded serious to me, and the operator hurriedly continued. "Mr. Charles Lowe is trying to get in touch with you! He says it's an emergency!"

I said, "Well, put him on," and while I was waiting all sorts of thoughts flashed through my mind. Something terrible must have happened to Carol. When Charlie got on the line he could hardly talk. "George," he gasped, "you better get over here right away! Carol might not be able to go on tonight, her wig shrunk!" And he hung up.

I stood there stunned. I thought to myself, How can a wig

shrink? Mine doesn't shrink. If you wear them too long, they stretch, but they never shrink. And I ought to know, I've got trunksful of hair. In fact, I got one trunk I part in the middle—but-wigs-just-don't-shrink!

Well, I caught a cab and rushed over to The Dunes. When I got to their room, there was Charlie on the phone frantically trying to reach somebody in the hair business, and there sat Carol almost in tears, holding a pathetic little wig in her hands.

I said to her, "What happened?"

She poured out this sad story: "I noticed my wig was getting a little dirty, so I washed it with soap and water. Then I put it out in the sun to dry—and it shrunk!" Carol had stumbled on the one way in the world that would make a wig shrink.

I knew that she would never go onstage without that wig, because her own hair was too short. And that wild blond hair was Carol's trademark and an important part of her act. Somehow we had to get her into that wig. I had Charlie stand on one side of her, and I stood on the other. Then we both took hold of the wig and stretched it open as far as we could. When Carol got her head into the wig we let go! If you think Carol's eyes are big, when that wig snapped on her head her eyes practically popped out and changed sockets. Frankly, I don't know how she went on and did two shows that night—but she did. And you know something? She was never better.

I've never known anyone with more energy than Carol has. And I think part of it is due to the organic food diet she's on. Everything Carol eats has to be specially prepared, so she always carries food around in her purse. You should get a load of that purse. It's filled with makeup, hair spray, pantyhose, her contact lenses, Kleenex, organic cookies, her own bottled water, and maybe even a buffalo steak or a moose cutlet wrapped in a napkin. She has to have energy just to be able to lift that purse.

Well, one night Judy Garland gave a special late show at

106

the Sahara Hotel for all the show people in town. So the five of us went—Charlie Reade, Charlie Lowe, Carol, the purse, and myself. Four of us ordered drinks, and Carol sat there munching on her moose cutlet. As usual, Judy was just marvelous, and after the show, as we were getting ready to go back and say hello, Carol said, "I'm going to tell Judy I love her, but she should do something about her makeup. It looked dark and streaky to me."

Charlie said, "Not to me. I thought she looked fine."

"I didn't think she looked dark and streaky," I said.

Carol sort of giggled and said, "Oh . . . I must have some gravy on my contact lenses."

I guess nobody looks good through moose gravy.

It was only natural that Carol went into show business, because of her family background. Not that her parents were performers, but they did spend the greater part of their lives appearing before audiences. Carol's father, George Channing, was the head lecturer for the Christian Science Church, and he traveled all over the world on speaking tours. He was also editor-in-chief of all Christian Science publications. He passed away in 1956 on the way back from one of his most successful tours. Carol's mother, Peggy Channing, was also very active in the church as a reader and practitioner, and as a matter of fact, still is.

I first met Mrs. Channing when Carol and I were playing The Dunes, and she had come to Las Vegas to visit Carol. She was a tall, beautiful, dignified, and charming lady of around seventy. When she arrived, Carol brought her into my dressing room to meet me, and after the introductions Carol returned to her dressing room to put on her makeup, leaving Mrs. Channing with me. There was an awkward pause during which neither one of us knew quite what to say, so I thought I'd use a little humor to ease the situation. She was wearing a short-sleeved dress, so I took her by the arm and said, "Sit down, Mrs. Channing." Before she could sit, I squeezed her arm and said, "Say, that's nice tight skin you've got there."

She just looked at me in complete disbelief.

I gave her arm another little squeeze and said, "Mrs. Channing, I hope you're not letting this nice tight skin go to waste."

I could feel the goose pimples popping up on her arm, but she just stood there looking at me, absolutely speechless. Then, attempting to melt her further, I said, "I know that your husband has been gone for six years, but if you're looking around, I know a young rabbi who's very anxious to get married."

Well, that did it. She pulled her arm away and literally flew out of the room. There I was, left with a handful of goose pimples. A minute later Carol came rushing in and said, "George, what in heaven's name did you say to my mother? She thinks I'm working with a crazy man!"

I said, "Carol, I was just trying to put her at ease."

Later on, when Mrs. Channing realized I was just having a little fun with her, we became good friends. I called her Peggy and she called me Mr. Burns. But now that I look back, she always arranged that we were never alone together.

During my entire career in show business I've never used dirty material—maybe a little risqué, but never what you'd call out and out dirty. And Carol was the same way. However, in our show at The Dunes we did do an opening routine that could be taken two ways. In Las Vegas it was perfectly acceptable and the audience loved it, but when we played Harrah's Club at Lake Tahoe we had a problem. Bill Harrah is a very straitlaced man and wanted us to take the routine out of our act because for his audience he thought it was off-color.

To give you an idea of what the controversy was all about, here's the way it went. After Carol and I sang a chorus of "This Could Be the Start of Something Big," we went into this routine:

108

GEORGE

Carol, you're a delight to work with because you're a great artist.

CAROL

Thank you, George. And it's a thrill to work with you because you've always been my idol. I've watched you work for years, and you've really got it.

GEORGE

I got it?

CAROL

Oh, yes.

GEORGE

I hope that's a compliment.

CAROL

Oh, it is. You know, to be a star some people have to be great singers, or great dancers, or great comedians, or great actors, but you made it without any of that.

GEORGE

But I got it.

CAROL

Oh, yes.

GEORGE

Well, Carol, what is this thing that I've got? Is it sort of a hidden talent?

CAROL

Oh, George, what you've got isn't hidden. Anybody can see it, it's right out in the open.

GEORGE

So before it catches cold—what would you say it is?

CAROL

Well, George, it's a certain something, and you've got it. You've not only got it, but you've always had it.

GEORGE
Let me see—it's something that I've got. Has Sinatra got it?

CAROL
Yes, but you've got twice as much.

GEORGE
Well, maybe it's because I'm older.

CAROL
Sure, so yours is developed more.

GEORGE
Now I'm really confused. How about Dean Martin, has he got it?

CAROL
Of course he's got it. But alongside of you, you can't even notice it.

GEORGE
Now this thing that I've got—and I've got twice as much as Sinatra—and when I'm with Dean Martin you don't notice his—has . . . has . . . has Richard Burton got it?

CAROL
Of course he's got it. And I know because Elizabeth Taylor happens to be a very close friend of mine.

GEORGE
This something that I've got, and I'm glad I got it—and I certainly wouldn't like to lose it—but I'd like to know what it is—can you describe it? Is it square? Is it round? Is it . . . is it as big as a breadbox?

CAROL
George, there's no way to measure it. You can't buy it, you can't sell it, you're born with it. You can't put your finger on it.

GEORGE
That maybe I've got. . . . Now, when did you find out I had it?

CAROL
The first time I ever saw you. You were playing the Palace

Theater and I was in the audience. The moment you walked out on the stage I said to the woman next to me, "He's got it."

GEORGE

What did the woman say?

CAROL

She said, "He must be hiding it, because I can't see it."

GEORGE

She couldn't see it, but you could?

CAROL

Well, that's because I'm in show business. I recognized it right away because I've seen it before.

GEORGE

Anyway, this something that I've got—at my age have I got enough of it left to last until the show is over?

CAROL

Why not? It's lasted all these years.

GEORGE

Well, whatever it is, it must be pretty tired by now. . . . One more question and I'll quit. Is there anybody else who's got as much of it as I have?

CAROL

Shirley MacLaine.

GEORGE

That I didn't expect. Georgie Jessel maybe, but Shirley MacLaine, never. . . .

CAROL

Oh, George, everybody in show business has got it.

GEORGE

Well, if I've still got it, I hope I don't lose it at the blackjack table. . . . Carol, it's time to finish our song.

Anyway, that's the routine, and Bill Harrah wanted it out. But Carol refused. She said to Harrah, "When I'm on

111

the stage all I'm talking about is George Burns' personality. If you're thinking of something else, then you're dirty, not the routine!"

Harrah came back with, "Well, if you're just talking about his personality, why is the audience laughing so hard?"

Very emphatically Carol said, "Because George Burns happens to have a very funny personality!"

Well, the routine stayed in. But we'd become so self-conscious about it that it lost all its humor, and after a few days we took it out. Bill Harrah had won.

In January of 1963, when John F. Kennedy was our President, the Democratic party gave a star-studded gala in Washington to celebrate the second anniversary of his inauguration. Carol and I were still working together, and we were both invited to Washington to entertain at the celebration. Naturally I took my road manager, Charlie Reade, with me.

Well, the affair was a tremendous success, and afterward we all went to Vice President Lyndon Johnson's house for a late supper. The place was full of Washington dignitaries and show business personalities, and all in all it was a very exciting evening. When I finally got back to my hotel, Charlie Reade was waiting for me and we packed our bags because we were due to fly out in the morning.

But it didn't happen. The next morning the Washington airport was fogged in and stayed that way all day. I finally got word that all flights had been canceled and we would have to leave early the following morning. So that night I decided that Charlie and I would just have dinner sent up to our rooms and we'd sit around and watch television. At about 6:30 I got into my pajamas, fixed a couple of drinks, and ordered our dinner. In the meantime Charlie had found a full-length mirror in the living room. And that's all Charlie needed. There he stood, in nothing but his jockey shorts and shoes, dancing his heart out and watching himself in

112

the mirror. Like I said, I love to watch Charlie dance, so I took my double martini, made myself comfortable, and sat there being entertained by one of the original Dunhills.

Right about then in rushed Carol Channing's husband, Charlie Lowe. He was all excited and out of breath. "George," he gasped, "the President's secretary just called, and the President couldn't make it back to Hyannisport because of the fog, so at the last minute he decided to hold a little dinner party at the White House!"

I said, "Good. That's where he lives—where else would he hold it?"

Charlie Lowe wasn't ready for any feeble attempts at humor. He blurted on, "George, you don't understand—*we're* invited! You and Carol and myself and our piano player! And we're supposed to be there in a half hour!"

"Not me," I said. "I'm not walking out in the middle of one of Charlie Reade's best routines."

Charlie Lowe was ready to have a fit. "George, this is no time to clown around!"

"But I'm all packed," I said to him. "I'm in my pajamas. And besides, I've already ordered my dinner."

With an icy look he said, "George, you don't turn down an invitation from the President of the United States. We'll meet you in the lobby in a half hour!" And he walked out.

During all this Charlie Reade hadn't stopped dancing. And after I got dressed and was ready to leave, he was still dancing.

Well, it turned out to be quite an evening at the White House. When we arrived we were met by Secret Service men who were to take us upstairs to the Kennedy living quarters. I can still remember that long walk down the hallway to the elevator in that big empty White House. You could hear the echo of your footsteps, and it made me think of Charlie Reade—he would have loved that floor.

As we entered their private living quarters, the President and Mrs. Kennedy were standing by the fireplace having a cocktail, so we joined them. Shortly the other guests arrived, and after we finished our cocktail we all went into dinner. There were nine of us: the President and Mrs. Kennedy; the British Ambassador, Sir David Ormsby-Gore, and his wife; Jacqueline Kennedy's sister, Lee Radziwell; Carol and Charlie Lowe; Bob Hunter, their piano player; and myself.

I was a little nervous when I sat down at the table because I was expecting a formal silver service, with all those different knives and forks and spoons. When I see all that silver it confuses me; I never know which end to start from. But that night all they had were two forks, a knife and a spoon. The two forks almost threw me, but I figured it out—the short one was for the salad.

It was just the kind of dinner I like—very simple. There was onion soup, a little green salad, a minute steak with some French peas, and dessert and coffee. And the whole dinner was served by one man. I've been to dinner parties in Hollywood where for nine people they had ten butlers. One is a standby in case one of the regular butlers burns his thumb in the soup.

During dinner the President and Sir Ormsby-Gore got into a discussion about the problems of putting a man on the moon. Well, I wasn't going to sit there like a dummy, so I got into the conversation without even waiting for an opening. I said, "Mr. President, I'm a member of the Hillcrest Country Club, and every day at the Round Table I have lunch with people like Groucho Marx, Georgie Jessel, Jack Benny, Danny Thomas, Danny Kaye, Lou Holtz, Jimmy Durante—and we're all good Americans. Now, whenever you get a problem like this just throw it our way and we'll be glad to iron it out for you." There was a second of silence, then the President started to laugh. Then Sir Ormsby-Gore laughed, although he didn't know why. And then everybody at the table started to laugh except Lee Radziwill. She never could figure out who I was.

After dinner we all went into the living room. Bob Hunter sat down at the piano and started noodling, and all of a sudden it was show time. The President asked Carol to sing "Diamonds Are a Girl's Best Friend," and she followed that with "I'm Just a Little Girl from Little Rock." Again I didn't want to sit there like a dummy, so I got up without even being asked. I opened with "Red Rose Rag," then went into "Willie, the Weeper, Was a Chimney Sweeper" and finished with "Strut, Miss Lizzie." Everybody applauded except Lee Radziwill. She not only couldn't figure out who I was, she couldn't figure out what I was.

For an encore I did my French version of "La Vie En Rose." Well, this broke Jacqueline Kennedy up completely. She said, "George, I've been speaking French all my life, and now after listening to you I find out I've been doing it all wrong."

After that everybody got into the act, and we had sort of a little impromptu songfest. It turned out to be such a relaxed fun evening we forgot where we were—sitting in the White House singing along with the President of the United States.

Around eleven o'clock, when we were getting ready to leave, the President asked us if we'd like to see Lincoln's bedroom. Naturally we all said yes, so we followed the President down the hall. He started into a room, then stepped back and quietly closed the door. He turned to us and said, "I'm sorry, I forgot that my mother is sleeping in there."

As we started back down the hall, Mrs. Kennedy whispered to Carol and myself, "I knew Rose was sleeping in Lincoln's bed. But he's the President, so I let him make his own mistakes."

Anyway, when the four of us got back to the hotel we were all so stimulated from the evening we decided to have a nightcap at the bar. Carol was bubbling all over and couldn't stop talking. "What a night," she said. "Imagine having dinner at the White House and singing harmony with the President of the United States! Nothing in the world can ever top this evening!"

I stood up and said, "Well, for me the evening is just beginning. When I get upstairs there'll be Charlie Reade standing in front of the mirror in his jockey shorts, doing a triple-time step. Good night, everybody." With that I walked away and left them sitting there in dead silence.

When I got up to my room the phone was ringing. It was Carol. "George," she said, "tell Charlie Reade to put on a robe, we're all coming up." And they did. We all sat around and watched Charlie dance. It's the first time one of the Dunhills ever followed the President of the United States.

Carol Channing and Charlie Lowe are still two of my closest friends, and whenever Carol has a new piece of material that she's going to do on the stage she always tries it out on me. She knows I've been in show business all my life, so she's sure I'll laugh in the right spots. And not to disappoint her, I always do. I'd do anything for Mrs. Charles Lowe.

No More Applause

On August 27, 1964, Gracie passed away.

I was terribly shocked, I just couldn't believe it—it all happened so suddenly. It was true that three years before, Gracie had a severe heart attack, but afterward she came out of the hospital and was just fine. For a short time we had round-the-clock nurses, but she improved so rapidly that we dismissed two of them and kept one as a nurse-companion for Gracie during the day. From time to time Gracie had little heart flutters, but this created no particular problem, because when the nurse wasn't there I knew exactly what to do. I knew where the pills were and which pill to give her. So when she had flareups, I'd give her the pill, put my arms around her, and we'd hold each other until it passed. It usually lasted no longer than a few seconds.

After a few months we treated this whole thing very casually. We got used to living with it. As long as I had the pills with me, we lived a very normal life. I remember one night we went to a party at Vincente Minnelli's house. It was a large party, and we were having a marvelous time. I had just finished singing three or four of my songs and was at the bar having a drink when Gracie came up to me and very quietly said, "I think we better step into the other room, I need one of my pills."

So we went into another room, I gave her a pill, we held on to each other, and it passed. After it was over, Gracie said, "I feel fine, but I think I'd be more comfortable at home." So I took her home. When we got there she insisted that I go back to the party, but gave me strict orders to keep

117

my eyes and ears open and watch everything that went on. "When you get home I want to hear everything that happened," she told me.

Back to the party I went, and I got home around midnight. There was Gracie sitting up in bed and waiting for me. She said, "Hurry up, get out of your clothes and come to bed. I want to hear every detail about the party."

Well, actually, all we did at the party was dance a little, have a few drinks, and sit around and talk. I had a perfectly fine time, but nothing out of the ordinary took place. But Gracie was sitting there primed for all the gossip, and I just couldn't disappoint her. From midnight to two in the morning I did nothing but make up a lot of lies about the wild and naughty things that went on at that party. I was in such good form that Gracie believed every word I said. In fact, I was so convincing I started to believe it myself. When I was all through, Gracie said, "Goodness, if I had known it was going to be that kind of a party, I certainly would have stayed."

Well, we finally turned off the lights and went to sleep. But about three in the morning Gracie nudged me awake. I turned over, still half asleep, and said, "What is it, Gracie?"

"Tell me again what Greg Bautzer said to that little starlet?" she begged.

I said, "Good night, Gracie"—I couldn't remember my lie.

This gives you an idea how casually we treated Gracie's illness. Those pills made me feel very secure. I figured we could go on this way year after year—it never entered my mind that anything would change it. Then one evening Gracie had another one of her attacks. I gave her the pill, we held on to each other—but this time it didn't work. When the pain continued, I called Dr. Kennamer, and they rushed Gracie to the hospital. . . . Two hours later Gracie was gone.

At first I couldn't accept it. I sat there stunned. I turned to Dr. Kennamer and said, "Doctor, how could this happen? I've still got pills left."

The doctor didn't say a word; he quietly ushered the other members of the family out of the room and left me there with Gracie. It was then that the full impact hit me. I knew I was alone.

There is a finality about death that is frightening, but there is nothing we can do about it. As difficult as it may be, we must all eventually realize that there's only one exit, and sooner or later every one of us has to make it. But life goes on in spite of everything, and now I had to build a whole new existence for myself. It wasn't easy—the period of adjustment to such a loss took time. Gracie had been such an all-important part of my life that everywhere I looked, everywhere I went, the feeling of her was still there. My family and friends did all they could to help me, but my days still seemed empty. For me, the most difficult time was at night. It was hard for me to go to sleep, and when I did doze off I'd soon wake with a start and look over, expecting Gracie to be there in her bed beside me.

This went on for about six months, then one night I did something, and to this day I can't explain why. I was all ready to get into bed, and then for some reason I pulled the covers down on Gracie's bed and got into it. I don't know whether it made me feel closer to her, or what it was, but for the first time since Gracie had gone I got a good night's sleep. I never did go back to my bed.

I didn't realize it at the time, but this proved to be the beginning of the end of my deep mourning period. Slowly I started returning to a more normal way of life; I began going out to dinner with my friends—I'd have people over to my house—I got interested in playing bridge again—I found myself buying new clothes—I even started going to the club and trading jokes with the fellows at the Round Table. At the time I was producing and appearing in a television series called "Wendy and Me" with Connie Stevens, and I was actually looking forward to going to work again. As I said, life does go on in spite of everything, and it did for me.

One thing I learned from all this is how strong the human spirit really is. Our ability to bounce back from what might

119

seem like the end of the world is absolutely amazing. And age has nothing to do with it. Whether you're eighteen or eighty, and whether you like it or not, you're going to go right on living.

I don't mean to imply that we can forget our loved ones who have passed on. I certainly never forgot Gracie, and I never will. She's in a mausoleum at Forest Lawn Memorial Park, and for the first year I used to take her flowers and visit her every week. The second year it was every two weeks, and after that and to this day I visit her once a month. When I first started these visits I'd put the flowers in front of the crypt and then sit there and cry and cry—I just couldn't stop. But there came a time when there were no more tears. I discovered that there are just so many tears one can cry and that crying is not going to change a thing.

I started talking to Gracie. Every time I'd visit her I'd tell her things; things about my work, things about our family, our friends, the plans that I had, etc. I don't know whether she heard me, but I like to think that she did. Later on it got so I'd tell her some of the funny things that happened to me. If I went to a party, I'd tell about all the amusing things that went on, but I made sure I always told her the truth. I figured she'd know if I was lying again.

When I was being considered for a part in the MGM movie *The Sunshine Boys,* I told Gracie all about it. I told her how I read for Neil Simon, who wrote the script, and Herb Ross, the director. I explained to her how I thought I gave a very good reading and that it was a great part, and how I knew if I got the chance I'd be able to do it. After I told her all this I said, "Gracie, maybe you can help, maybe you can put in a good word for me up there. But don't bother the head man, he's very busy. Talk to his son, and be sure to tell him I'm Jewish, too." This time she must have heard me—I did get the part.

Thank You, Mr. Toastmaster . . .

In the business I'm in I'm constantly being called on to make speeches at various functions. That not only goes for me, but applies to Milton Berle, Don Rickles, Buddy Hackett, Joey Bishop, Jan Murray, Nipsey Russell, Steve Allen, George Jessel, Jack Carter, Dean Martin, Johnny Carson, and many others. If I accepted all the after-dinner speeches I'm asked to make, I'd spend half of my life eating chicken croquettes and sitting between Milton Berle and Jack Carter.

Somebody is always calling me on the telephone and saying, "George, we're giving a testimonial dinner for so-and-so Friday night and the evening wouldn't be complete without you on the dais. All you have to do is get up and only do five or six minutes." Have you any idea how long five or six minutes can be? Tonight before dinner why don't you try it; stand up at the table and talk to your wife for six minutes—and try to get laughs while you're doing it.

I don't think people realize how much work and preparation it takes to prepare a six-minute speech. In the first place, when you write it, it has to be tailored to fit the guest of honor. You play off of his personality traits—things he's known for—his physical characteristics, etc. I remember once I was asked to speak at a dinner honoring Kirk Douglas. Now, one of his most discernible physical characteristics is a dimple in his chin, so naturally I wrote two or three minutes of dimple jokes. Then I got to thinking—everybody on the dais would be doing dimple jokes, so I figured

I'd outwit them. I threw out all my dimple jokes and concentrated on Kirk Douglas' multiple talents: acting, writing, producing, directing, etc. At the night of the affair what happened? Everybody had been trying to outwit everybody else; they'd all thrown out their dimple jokes and talked about Kirk's multiple talents. He was very upset. There he sat with this beautiful dimple and nobody mentioned it.

Not only does it take hours to write these five or six minutes, in my case it takes hours to memorize them. As a rule everyone on the dais has his speech written out on little cards and he reads it. I used to do that too, but I learned my lesson.

They gave Georgie Raft a dinner one night and I was sitting next to Milton Berle. While I was eating my chicken croquettes Milton stole my cards. What he forgot was that he and I don't work anything alike, so when he got up and did my speech he didn't get any laughs. Afterward he came over to me, slammed the cards down on the table, and said, "George, you better get yourself a new writer!" I didn't feel too bad. While he was doing my speech I stole his chicken croquettes. That's the last time I ever used cards—and it's also the last time I ate a chicken croquette.

I'd say that over the years I've made most of my speeches for the Friars Club, both here and in New York. I've belonged to the New York Friars for over fifty years, and the one out here since it was founded. They're theatrical clubs, and most of the proceeds from these functions go to worthy charities.

The Friars are famous for their "roasts," which are always stag affairs. A well-known personality is chosen to be the guest of honor, and then they literally tear him to pieces by insulting him with the dirtiest and filthiest language possible. I used to do these roasts quite frequently, but now I've stopped doing them; I don't think they're fun anymore. After all, everyone gets up and uses the same dirty words, and how many dirty words are there? In the entire English

122

language there are only thirty-one dirty words—wait a minute, I just thought of another one—make that thirty-two.

Some of the people they roast aren't easy to talk about; they're just not colorful; they don't have any characteristics or traits that you can make jokes about. Can you imagine getting up and doing six funny minutes on Calvin Coolidge?

A good example of this happened to me when I was asked to speak at a dinner honoring General Omar Bradley. I didn't know where to begin. I tried several approaches, but nothing seemed to come out funny. I was about to call up and tell them I couldn't make it when out of the blue my show-business genius rescued me. (My show-business genius was one of my writers.) It was so simple I almost fired my show-business genius for not thinking of it sooner. What I did was take the very thing that was stumping me and turned it into a plus.

The dinner for General Bradley was held at a theatrical club, the Masquers, and Pat Buttram was the toastmaster. This was my speech:

Thank you, Pat, for that nice introduction. Excuse me while I light my cigar. I can't talk unless I smoke. Seeing me without a cigar would be like offering Pat Buttram a drink and having him say, "No, thank you." . . . I must smoke about twenty or thirty cigars a day. The older I get the more I smoke. When I was eighteen I only smoked one cigar a day. Of course, in those days I was able to do other things. I've reached the stage now that I can't even remember what those other things were. But you know, it's comfortable when you get to the point where you just smoke cigars and do nothing else. In the first place, you don't have to get undressed to smoke a cigar. And when you're finished with a cigar you don't have to call a cab to take it home.

And now to our distinguished guest of honor, General Omar Bradley. You know, I'm in a very funny spot tonight. I really don't know what to say. I've met the General, but we

123

really have very little in common. He's a five-star general, and I'm a singer. I've never shot a gun, and I'm sure he doesn't know the verse to "Some of These Days." I've never been in the Army or the Navy, the Marines, the Air Corps. In fact, the Boy Scouts wouldn't even take me. But I felt I should do something for my country, so I joined the Girl Scouts. I got away with it for about two months until one night in the locker room after a basketball game. I thought they were going to throw me out, but the woman in charge of the troop took a look at me and said, "Let him stay, he's not going to hurt anybody." At that time I was a so-prano. . . .

Anyway, when Harry Joe Brown, your program director, asked me to speak here tonight, I said to him, "Harry, you got the wrong fellow. It's not easy for me to talk about anybody unless I've been close to him. So you better count me out."

Harry said, "George, everybody on the dais is going to be talking about the General. You can be different. Do four minutes of show-business anecdotes, you know a million of them." I said, "Do you think it will work?" He said, "Of course, but one thing—the General is a very distinguished man, and there will be ladies in the audience, so don't get risqué, just do four warm and humorous minutes."

So I said, "Harry, do you think I can tell this one? It's about Georgie Jessel being married four times. In those days he considered himself a great lover, and he was—but not at home. And his four wives left him, and I don't blame them. It must be very uncomfortable to be married to a guy who goes to bed wearing all those medals, they couldn't get any sleep, all night long he tinkled."

Harry said, "George, that's a funny joke, but not in front of the General. Forget the four minutes, do about three min-utes—three, nice, clean, warm minutes will be plenty."

I said, "Well, can I tell the one about Jack Benny before he was married and he was running around with this girl Lily DeFore who was working at Leon and Eddie's? She did this act where she painted her whole body gold. Jack and I were living together at the time, and one night when we were get-ting ready to go to bed I said, "Jack, is there anything going on between you and Lily?" Jack said, "No, George, absolutely nothing." Then he turned out the lights, and the glow from his underwear kept me awake all night."

Harry said, "George, the General is in the Army and he's not used to risque things like that. Two minutes will be plenty. Believe me, at these affairs the shorter you keep it the better they like you."

I said, "Well, it won't be easy, Harry, but as long as I've only got two minutes I better tell one of my really good ones. I'll do the one about the girl I worked on the bill with in Altoona. She was a great performer. She could bend over backwards till her head touched the floor, and then she'd take both of her legs and wrap them around her neck. And she did some great stuff on stage, too. . . ."

Harry said, "Hold it, George, just do one minute . . . some short, cute little story, something that happened to you when you were a kid."

I said, "Oh, yeah, I've got a beauty. I was in the third grade, and my teacher, Mrs. Hollander, told me about the birds and the bees. I couldn't believe my ears. Those sweet little birds and those darling little bees, to think of them doing what my sister Goldie was doing was just shocking. . . . That was sixty-eight years ago, and all those birds and bees are dead now, but my sister Goldie is still trying. . . . That's not shocking, that's hopeless."

Harry said, "George, just do thirty seconds. Say something nice about the General for thirty seconds."

I said, "All right, I can tell about the only time I met him. It was at Hillcrest Country Club and he was there for lunch. Naturally we were all impressed. Then I got up and went into the men's room, and I was standing there when the General came in and stood next to me. I got so nervous I didn't know what to do, so I saluted him and ruined a perfectly good pair of shoes."

Harry said, "George, I've got an idea. There will be so many people on the dais that there's really no reason for you to show up. The next time you run into General Bradley, just wave to him."

I said, "Harry, I'd love to wave to him, but I'm afraid I might ruin another pair of shoes."

That's when Harry Joe left. I think I'm going to leave, too. I'm sorry, General, I did my best.

I thought the speech went very well, but later on I was standing at the bar having a drink when I noticed the General walking toward me. He wasn't smiling, so I didn't know what to expect. He put his hand on my shoulder and said, "George, I want to thank you for being here tonight, and I love the way you cleaned up that speech."

I relaxed a bit and said, "Thank you, General, and I'm glad you enjoyed it."

The General smiled a big smile and said, "I really did, George." Then, with just a twinkle in his eyes—"And if you ever think of joining the Army, I'll see that you get a new pair of shoes."

As he walked away, I couldn't help but compare him with Georgie Jessel. Jessel goes around with his chest covered with medals, and here's this great five-star general and he doesn't tinkle at all. I can say things like that about Jessel, and he can say anything he wants about me, because our friendship goes back a lot of years.

I could have saved myself a lot of time and worry about my approach to the General Bradley speech if I had just gone through my files. While preparing this chapter I discovered I used practically the same format at a testimonial dinner The Friars gave for Georgie Jessel back in 1948. I found out then that you can do a dirty speech without using one dirty word. You innocently plant a seed in the audience's mind, and when they read something dirty into it, you act as though you're shocked that this naughty audience could even think of such a thing. And the more shocked you look the funnier the speech gets.

Anyway, here's the Jessel speech:

Brother Friars, ladies and gentlemen, toastmaster and guest of honor, George Jessel. Well, another Friars' dinner, and on the dais practically the same faces. There's Jessel, Jolson, Cantor, Benny, Danny Kaye, Pat O'Brien, and Bob Hope. You'll notice I'm giving Pat O'Brien and Bob Hope bottom billing. If they were Jewish, I'd move them up front with us boys. . . .

Now to our guest of honor. I've known Georgie Jessel for years. I remember when he was starring in *The Jazz Singer* on Broadway. Jessel was a tremendous hit, but when they made the movie of *The Jazz Singer* Warner Brothers hired Al Jolson to star in it, and naturally this upset Jessel. He thought he should star in the movie because he originated that part. In fact, Jessel was so mad he took an oath that he'd break the Warner Brothers if it took his last cent. And I know exactly how much money Georgie Jessel has got left, so the Warner Brothers should be broke by this Thursday. . . .

Well, that's the end of my speech. I'm sorry, but I must tell you what happened. I didn't know there was going to be a mixed audience here tonight. I put together a lot of funny stuff about Jessel, but I can't use any of it. Don't you think that somebody would have told me that this was not going to be a stag affair? Who'd ever figure they'd throw a clean dinner for Jessel. . . .

Wait a minute, maybe I can take that speech of mine and clean it up as I go along. This isn't going to be easy, but I'll try.

I remember when Jessel went on the road with *The Jazz Singer* and he was playing Cleveland. There was this pretty girl who saw Jessel in the play and went for him in a big way. Well, one night Jessel invited her up to his suite at the Statler Hotel. I was in town playing the Keith Theater, so I thought I'd surprise Georgie. After the show I went up to his hotel room. Now when a guy's got a dame in his room doing what Jessel usually— Well, wouldn't you think he'd lock the door? But he didn't, so I walked right in, and there was Jessel with his— That I can't clean up.

A year later he went back into vaudeville and was booked on the Orpheum circuit. He opened in Minneapolis, and on the bill was this beautiful sister act. Well, Jessel invited one of the sisters out for dinner after the show. As you know, it gets very cold in Minneapolis, and after dinner when they

127

went back to the hotel there was no heat because the furnace had broken down. The girl said, "Georgie, can't you do something, I'm freezing?" Well, Jessel thought he'd warm things up for her, so he—

Then he played Winnipeg. . . . And in Winnipeg he was on the bill with a girl act called Lasky's Redheads—eight gorgeous showgirls. And one night he got all eight girls up into his suite and he—

Then he played Vancouver. . . . In Vancouver there was a little restaurant right alongside the theater, and there was this very sexy blond waitress—

From there he went to Seattle. . . . There he met this beautiful Chinese girl who was a stripper at the Primrose Pagoda— Then he played Portland. . . .

Then San Francisco . . .

Oakland . . .

Los Angeles . . .

Tijuana . . .

This is silly, there must be something clean I can say about Jessel. . . . Let's go back to his childhood. When Georgie Jessel was eight years old—

No, I didn't go back far enough. . . .

I'm sorry, I can't do this speech in front of a mixed audience. Later on I'll be glad to tell it to you ladies alone. . . .

Thank you very much.

Well, that speech turned out to be the hit of the evening. I never got such laughs. I really was elated. I sat there complimenting myself how I was able to make a speech like that without using one of those thirty-two words. But this ego trip didn't last too long. A matronly woman came up to me and, clutching my hand, said, "Mr. Burns, you're an amazing man. Only you could get away with a dirty speech like that in mixed company."

I didn't know what to think. I asked her, "What did I say tonight that was so off-color?"

The woman gave sort of a kittenish giggle and said, "Oh, Mr. Burns, I don't use words like that," and ran off.

There you are, this woman thought she heard me say

things that I never said, and all because I planted that little seed. It really works.

As we were all leaving later on, Lucille Ball grabbed me by the arm and pulled me aside. "George," she said, "my husband's ashamed to ask you this, but I'm not. What did Jessel do with that Chinese girl in Seattle?"

I said, "Lucy, they spent a very exciting evening—they sat around reading fortune cookies."

She gave me one of those looks, and said, "George Burns, you're the dirtiest man I know!"

But the most elegant affair I was ever invited to speak at was a testimonial dinner for Alfred Lunt and Lynn Fontanne at The Players Club in New York City. The Players is a very sophisticated theatrical club, and the membership consists of important actors, writers, producers, directors, etc., from the legitimate theater. To give you an idea of how distinguished the occasion was, besides myself here are the speakers who were on the dais that night: Sir John Gielgud, Sir Ralph Richardson, Peter Ustinov, Howard Lindsay, Russel Crouse, Marc Connelly and, of course, Alfred Lunt and Lynn Fontanne. Now, if you're wondering how a small-time vaudeville actor like me wound up in that kind of company, pull up a chair and I'll tell you.

Gracie and I had always been big fans of Alfred Lunt and Lynn Fontanne, but we had never met them. To us they were like the Royal Family of the theater, and we felt that they were way out of our league. Then, one night years ago in Beverly Hills, we were having a dinner party for ten people, and Carol Channing and her husband, Charlie Lowe, were two of the guests. At the last minute Carol called up Gracie and said, "I know this is an imposition, Gracie, but we're with Alfred Lunt and Lynn Fontanne, and I was wondering if we could bring them to dinner with us."

Gracie nearly dropped the phone. "Of course," she stammered, "you can bring them, we'll be delighted." Then she dropped the phone and came running breathlessly into the den, saying, "George . . . George, guess what's happened!

129

Carol just called and she's bringing Alfred Lunt and Lynn Fontanne to dinner!"

I looked at her and said, "You're kidding! Do you think we have time to have the house painted?"

"This is no time to be funny, George," Gracie snapped. "I'm going up to change my dress," and out she ran.

I don't mind telling you I was just as nervous as she was. I'd been making myself a martini, and I immediately turned it into a double. What do you say to people like them?

But as it turned out, there was nothing to be nervous about. When the Lunts arrived, the first thing Alfred did was hit Gracie with one of her lines that he remembered out of our first vaudeville act. In a perfect imitation of Gracie, he said, "I'm glad I'm dizzy boys like dizzy girls and I like boys and you must be glad I'm dizzy because you're a boy and I like boys!"

I don't know how he remembered that line, but it certainly broke the ice. Everybody relaxed, and we had a marvelous evening—until it was time for dinner. In the excitement Gracie had forgotten to tell our help that there would be two more place settings at the table. So when we all walked into the dining room there we were, twelve people with only ten chairs. It got pretty confusing—no matter how Gracie arranged the seating there were always two people left standing. Finally Gracie realized what had happened. "Oh, my goodness," she said, "I'm so embarrassed, I forgot the Lunts!"

The Lunts laughed, and Alfred said, "Don't worry about it, Gracie, we can always eat standing up."

And Lynn added, "Relax, Gracie, I've been married to Alfred long enough to know he likes dizzy girls." So we got two more chairs, and it was a very memorable evening.

Well, that's how we met the Lunts, and two years later it resulted in me being invited to speak at their testimonial dinner at The Players. It turned out to be quite a nerve-racking evening for me. I sat there on the dais as one after the other of these theater greats got up and made eloquent speeches extolling the Lunts and their place in the theater. Finally I realized that everyone on the dais had been called upon except me. I thought that Howard Lindsay, the toastmaster, had forgotten I was there. But he hadn't. He had saved me for the last speaker before he introduced the Lunts, which was very flattering. But it was also a little frightening. Remember, most of the people there that night had never even seen a vaudeville actor.

Well, this was my speech:

Members of The Players club, distinguished guests on the dais, toastmaster Howard Lindsay, and guests of honor, Alfred Lunt and Lynn Fontanne. First, I'd like to apologize for having this makeup on. I just came from taping a show for Jack Paar, and I was a smash. I sang some of the songs I made famous, like "Tiger Girl," and "The Heart of a Cherry," and "I'll Be Waiting for You, Bill, When You Come Back from San Juan Hill." . . .

I love to sing. You know, every night when Gracie and I go to bed I sing her seven or eight songs until she falls asleep. And it works. We've been happily married for thirty-seven years. At my age it's easier to sing. . . . And if our guest of honor, Alfred Lunt, is having the same problem, I'll be glad to teach him a few choruses of "Tiger Girl." . . .

Excuse me while I light my cigar. I can't talk unless I smoke. Seeing me without a cigar would be like seeing Sir John Gielgud playing on the same bill with Fink's Mules. . . .

What a pleasure it is to see Howard Lindsay as toastmaster. For the last fifteen years I've been looking at Georgie Jessel. Not that Jessel isn't a great toastmaster, he is. But after he gets through calling you every dirty name in the book, you've got to buy a bond for Israel. . . . You see, I'm a member of the Friars Club and I make a lot of speeches there, but it's always stag. So if I look a little nervous up here, it's not that I don't know what to say, but this just isn't the place to say it. In fact, I couldn't even say it in your men's room. This is such a high-class affair tonight that even the attendant in the men's room is wearing dinner clothes. He wouldn't give

131

me a towel to wipe my hands until I told him my name was Sir George Burns.

Let me tell you a little about myself. I never played a good theater until I met Gracie. Before that I was a small-time vaudeville actor until I was twenty-seven years old. You should have seen some of the broken-down theaters I played. I played one theater that was so bad "Madame Burkhardt and Her Cockatoos" were the headliners. I was just unbelievably bad, but who cared, I wanted to be in show business and I was. I had to change my name every week; I could never get a job with the same name twice. I was Jack Harris of Harris & Kelly. I was Phil Baxter of Baxter & Bates. I was Davis of Delight and Davis—my name was Sammy Davis. . . . Don't look so shocked—I was Jewish before he was, too. I used so many different names it got to the point where I didn't know who I was.

I remember one of the first acts I ever did was a singing, dancing and rollerskating act—Brown and Williams. Sid Brown and Harry Williams. . . . I don't remember whether I was Brown or Williams, but we got into a fight and split up the act. We both got different partners but did the same act. So now you had Brown and Williams and Williams and Brown. Then the four of us split up, got different partners, and again we all did the same act. Now we had Brown and Williams, Williams and Brown, Brown and Brown, and Williams and Williams. Then came another split. Now you had Brown and Williams, Williams and Brown, Brown and Brown, Williams and Williams, the Brown Brothers, and the Williams Boys. By the time we got through, every Jewish person on the East Side was either named Brown or Williams. There was one kid, Hymie Goldberg, he moved. He said he was afraid to live in a gentile neighborhood.

Then I did a ballroom dancing act called Pedro Lopez and Conchita. My name was Pedro Lopez. Conchita's real name was Lila Berkowitz, but I used to smoke those little Conchita cigars, so I named her after the cigar. . . . We were booked into the Farley Theater in Brooklyn, and to give you an idea of how bad we were, the music for our opening number was "La Czarina," which is a Russian mazurka. We thought it was a Spanish dance, so we wore Spanish outfits. I wore a little black bolero coat with a green sash around my waist, and I parted my hair in the middle and plastered it down with Vaseline. I wanted to look like Ramon Navarro. . . .

Conchita had a red Spanish shawl with gold fringe around it, which she'd fasten under one arm, leaving one shoulder bare. And she also wore one of those big, heavy Spanish combs in her hair. It used to press on a nerve in her head and drove her crazy—they finally had to take her away. . . . She wore an evening dress under the shawl, and for our second number she'd pull the shawl off and put her arm in the sleeve of the dress. Then she'd pick up a fan, and she was ready. I'd pull off my sash, put on a top hat, grab my cane, and we were ready to do our next number, which was a Cakewalk.

At this one particular performance that comb was pressing on Conchita's nerve, and she didn't know what she was doing. She picked up the fan okay, but when she took off the shawl she forgot to put her arm in her sleeve. Well, when we started the Cakewalk, which is a very bouncy number, with her arm out of her sleeve, one of her things kept flapping up against her chest. I thought it was the audience applauding, so I kept taking bows.

Our closing number was the Turkey Trot with a whirlwind finish. For this Conchita had changed into a white evening gown with just two thin straps. Now, Conchita came from the lower East Side, and in those days a lot of Jewish girls never shaved under their arms, so she had all this hair hanging down. When we started to pivot, with that comb pressing on her nerve and me stepping on her hair, poor Conchita was sorry she ever got into show business. And for our finish she'd put her arms around my neck and I'd spin her around in the air. It looked like I was swinging two rabbis. Anyway, before the week was over they took Conchita away, and I changed my name again.

Well, that's enough about the glamor of small-time vaudeville.

Now to our guests of honor, Alfred Lunt and Lynn Fontanne. In case you're wondering why I've spent so much time talking about small-time vaudeville, it's because I just don't know our guests of honor well enough to lie about them. They did come to our house about a year ago for sort

133

of a confused dinner, and the soup spoons they used . . . we haven't let anyone use them since. In fact, we had them bronzed.

Gracie and I always loved the Lunts. We've seen practically all of their shows for the last thirty years, and we've always sent them flowers. But we never went backstage to meet them. We never even thought that we belonged in their dressing room. And we certainly never played anyplace with the Lunts. They never played the Gus Sun Circuit, and we never played for the Theater Guild.

But I've thought it over, and I do have something in common with the Lunts. They've been in show business all their lives, and I've been in show business all my life. So if age counts, my billing is right up there with the Lunts.

Anyway, I'm thrilled that I was asked to speak here tonight. And before I sit down I'd like to say something to Lynn Fontanne. Lynn, if you're thinking of getting rid of that straight man you've been using, I've got a trunkful of stuff. I'd give anything to sing two choruses of *The Guardsman*. What a team we'd make—Lynn Fontanne and George Burns. You'll notice, of course, I'm even giving you top billing. Thank you very much.

Well, the members of The Players club were delighted with my speech, and a week later I got a telegram from the membership committee. It said that Alfred Lunt had suggested that they ask me to become a member of The Players. This was a very flattering gesture, and even though I don't play chess, shoot billiards, or drink my scotch and water without ice, I joined. I was a member for three years and never went near the place. Here I was, living in California and a member of two other theatrical clubs. It seemed silly to be paying dues to another club in New York, so I sent a telegram to the membership committee. I said, GENTLEMEN, I'D LIKE TO RESIGN FROM THE PLAYERS CLUB, BUT ONLY UNDER ONE CONDITION. PROMISE YOU DON'T TELL ALFRED LUNT. IF HE EVER FOUND OUT, HE'D MAKE ME REMOVE THE BRONZE FROM HIS SOUP SPOON. GEORGE BURNS.

The Quiet Riot

Somebody once said if you live long enough, sooner or later everything that can happen to you will happen. And it's true. However, I figure there must be sometime in life when you complete the cycle and start all over again. I wonder how old I'll be when I get the mumps again?

As you go through life, the good things and the bad things have a way of balancing themselves out. But there are times when you get the feeling that the bad things are winning. That's the way I felt the day my closest friend, Jack Benny, passed away. I was at the house with his family when word came down from upstairs that Jack was gone. I told Mary I'd like to go upstairs alone for a few moments and say goodbye to Jack. When I went into the room he was lying there with his hands clasped in that familiar manner and his head cocked to one side—he looked as though he were taking one of his long pauses.

Even though those of us close to Jack knew that his illness was terminal, when the end actually came we weren't ready for it. I've come to realize that death is forever, and there is no way one can completely accept it. I also realize that there is nothing one can do about it.

Jack was gone and part of me went with him, but a lot of Jack stayed here with me. Not only me—part of him stayed with people all over the world. Jack's image was so well established and the character he played was based on such reality that everybody thought of him as a personal friend.

Who could forget that walk, that voice, those familiar gestures, the outraged glances? Whenever one of Jack's self-provoked situations backfired we all suffered his humiliation right along with him. But we laughed while we did it.

That was Jack Benny the performer, the perennial thirty-nine-year-old tightwad. But the Jack Benny I knew was entirely different. He was really something special. He was the warmest and most considerate man I ever knew. Everybody who came in contact with Jack fell in love with him. And the feeling was mutual because Jack loved people. It didn't matter if they were rich, poor, tall, small, round, square, black, white, yellow or even burnt orange—Jack just loved people.

Many years ago in New York he did something that's a perfect example of what I'm talking about. He had a very important business meeting with some of the top NBC executives. Jack's manager, Irving Fein, was there also, and when Jack didn't show up on time, Irving started to get very nervous. Jack finally did arrive twenty minutes late. He apologized and explained that he had been downstairs talking to Charlie, the elevator starter. It seemed that Charlie's wife had just had a baby, and Jack was very excited about it. Irving and the NBC brass all listened to the story, and when Jack had finished, Irving said, "All right, Jack, now can we start the meeting?"

Jack said, "One more thing, Irving. On our way out remind me to ask Charlie what hospital his wife is in, I want to send her some flowers."

Then they started the meeting.

There were all kinds of little things Jack used to do that I wish I had done. I must admit I thought of them, but I never did them. A great deal of Jack's time was spent on the road making personal appearances and giving charity concerts for symphony orchestras. It was a hectic schedule, but he always found time to write fifty or sixty postcards every week. They were personal notes to his friends, and they al-

136

ways ended with some kind of a little joke. Jack had a secretary who traveled with him, but Jack wrote every one of those postcards in longhand. I'm sure he felt that a handwritten note made it more intimate and friendly. To him a typewritten note was something that came from a bank.

The longer I knew Jack the more he amazed me. Sometimes for no reason at all he would stop at a little bakery in Beverly Hills, buy a cake, and take it up to his doctor's office. The receptionist and the nurses would make coffee, and they'd all sit around and have a little gossip session. Jack didn't have an appointment with the doctor, he just got a kick out of talking to the girls.

Now, I'd love to do something like that, but I never would. I'd figure the girls would think I was doing it just because I wanted them to think I was trying to be nice. But that never entered Jack's mind. He was just naturally nice without trying.

I envied Jack because he enjoyed everything. In all the time I knew him there was just one little thing that always griped him. He could never get what he considered a good cup of coffee. He once said to me, "George, I've traveled all over the world, I've been everywhere at least once, and I've yet to find a good cup of coffee."

"Jack," I said, "if you've never tasted a good cup of coffee, how would you know if you got one?"

He gave me one of his scornful looks and said, "George, if that was supposed to be funny, it's lucky you don't make your living as a writer," and walked away.

But I think I figured out why the little things, even a cup of coffee, were just as important to Jack as the big things. He was a superstar for a lot of years and had achieved every goal it's possible to reach in show business. And when you've been on top for so many years, each major success loses its importance; you start thinking of each accomplishment as a daily routine.

Of course, when Jack was just getting started it was different. I remember when he first opened at The Palace theater in New York he was very nervous. The second time he played The Palace he was still nervous. But the third time he couldn't figure out why all the other actors were nervous. He got so used to being a hit at The Palace the only thing he worried about was whether the delicatessen next door would save him a piece of cheesecake after the show.

That's the way Jack was for the rest of his life. But sometimes those little things that thrilled him so got to be ludicrous. One day I ran into him coming out of the locker room at the club. Did he say "Hello" or "How are you?" No! He just blurted out, "George, did you take a shower today?"

I didn't know what to say; I thought maybe I had stepped in something. "Yeah, Jack, I took a shower at home this morning," I said.

"Well, you've got to take another one here," Jack urged. "I just took one and the towels are great! They're the softest, fluffiest towels I ever dried myself with!"

I just stood there and looked at him. How do you answer a thing like that? So I went into the card room. Later, when I was leaving, I passed Jack and Eddie Buzzell, and as I went by all I could hear was Jack saying, "Eddie, did you take a shower today?" I didn't look back, I ran out of the club.

There wasn't a day went by that Jack didn't come in on his toes bubbling with excitement over some new bit of trivia he'd discovered. With Jack the last thing that happened to him was always the greatest. One day he said, "George, I've just had the coldest glass of water I've ever had in my life!" Another time he said to me, "I just ate the most delicious bacon and tomato sandwich I ever tasted!" Once he interrupted me in the middle of a bridge game to tell me that Sammy in the locker room just gave him the greatest shoeshine he ever had in his life.

I usually ignored these earth-shaking discoveries of Jack's. I just passed them off as part of being Jack Benny's best friend. But once in a while he'd come up with something you just couldn't walk away from. One Sunday morning Jack and I were going to play nine holes of golf and we were having breakfast together at the club. After we gave our order Jack said to me, "I was with the world's greatest comedian last night."

"Who were you with?" I asked him.

Jack sensed that he was heading for trouble. He hemmed and hawed, and finally said, "Well. . . *you* might not think he's the world's greatest comedian."

From Jack's attitude I knew he had put his foot in it, so from there on I started playing with him. I said, "Well, maybe this fellow isn't the world's greatest comedian—maybe he's the world's second-greatest comedian. Who is he?"

Jack said, "George, look—it was what he said last night that made him sound like the world's greatest comedian."

"Jack, what did he say?"

Fighting for his life, Jack stammered, "Well . . . it . . . it . . . it isn't *what* he said, it's how he said it."

Taking dead aim, I said, "Jack, you're one of the great comedians, and you've got a great delivery—tell me the line, and if he made you laugh, I'm sure you'll make me laugh."

Jack said, "George, the line wouldn't be funny now. It was the situation last night that made the line funny."

I said, "Jack, I still would like to know who this great comedian is."

There was this long pause. Then, without daring to look at me, Jack said, "Larry Adler."

Now it was my turn to take a long pause. Finally I said, "Larry Adler, the harmonica player, is the world's greatest comedian?"

Trying to dig his way out, Jack said, "George, let me tell you exactly what happened. Last night we went to a party, and the entrance to the house was this big, heavy, iron gate.

Well, Larry Adler went through first, and as I came through that's when he said, 'Jack, don't slam the door.' "

I looked straight at him and said, "He must have said something else."

Irritably, Jack snapped, "That's it, George—'Don't slam the door'!"

I said, "And that line made you think that this harmonica player was the world's greatest comedian—'Don't slam the door'? Jack, if I were you, I wouldn't go around telling people that Larry Adler said that line. It might not be his. Maybe he stole it from Borrah Minnevitch!" I could have worked on Jack for another few minutes, but by this time he was rolling on the floor laughing.

It's been a well-known fact in show business that I could always make Jack Benny laugh. And it was always silly little things that would do it—things that nobody else would laugh at. During all the years I knew Jack I never told him an out-and-out joke, because that would be the last thing he'd laugh at. He made his living writing comedy, so if you told him a joke, first he'd analyze it, then he'd start to rewrite it.

Now, here's something I did at a party one night and it made Jack hysterical. You're not going to believe this, and I don't blame you because I still don't believe it either. It started while we were both standing at the bar having a drink. We were wearing dinner clothes, and I noticed that there was a little piece of white thread stuck on the lapel of Jack's coat. I said, "Jack, that piece of thread you're wearing on your lapel tonight looks very smart. Do you mind if I borrow it?" Then I took the piece of thread from his lapel and put it on my lapel.

That was it—that was the whole thing. I'm not sure, but I think that during my life in show business I must have thought of a funnier bit—I certainly hope so. But that bit of business took Jack apart. He laughed, he pounded the bar, he kept pounding the bar, and finally he collapsed on the floor, laughing. I must admit I always loved every moment

140

of it. Being able to send this great comedian into spasms of hysterical laughter was good for my ego.

Anyway, the next day I got a little box, put a piece of white thread in it, and sent it over to Jack's house with a note that said, "Jack, thanks for letting me wear this last night."

An hour later I got a phone call from Mary. She said, "George, that piece of white thread got here an hour ago and Jack is still on the floor. When he stops laughing I think I'll leave him!"

You know, over the years I'm surprised that Jack never got mad at me. When I think back, I really did some awful things. One night Norman Krasna gave a party, and before dinner there were about thirty or forty of us standing around having cocktails and hors d'oeuvres. The room was buzzing with the usual small talk, and I happened to glance across the room and noticed that Jack was taking a cigarette and a match out of a box on the mantelpiece. I held up my hands, and in a loud voice called out, "Quiet, everybody!" A hush fell over the room, and every eye turned to me. "Ladies and gentlemen," I said, "Jack Benny is now going to do his famous match bit!" Every eye now turned to Jack. There he stood, with a cigarette in one hand, a match in the other, and a bewildered expression on his face. He didn't know what to do; he just stood there squirming uncomfortably. After a few seconds he put the cigarette in his mouth and lit it. I said, "Jack, that's much better—I notice you've got a new finish!" Well, that did it. The cigarette flew out of his mouth; he almost fell into the fireplace and couldn't stop laughing.

There are many other awful things I did to Jack, but he loved them. He enjoyed them so much it became one of the big routines in his nightclub act. He'd stand up there and spend ten minutes telling the people what a miserable man I was. I think if I had been nice, I would never have been his best friend.

Once I was playing the Majestic Theater in Chicago, and

at the same time Jack was playing the Orpheum Theater in Milwaukee. His show closed on a Saturday night, so he decided to come to Chicago and spend Sunday with me. He sent a wire which read: AM ARRIVING CHICAGO 10:30 SUNDAY MORNING. MEET ME AT THE RAILROAD STATION.

I wired back: LOOKING FORWARD TO SEEING YOU. WHAT TIME ARE YOU ARRIVING I'D LIKE TO MEET YOU.

Jack wired me: AM ARRIVING SUNDAY MORNING AT 10:30.

I sent off another wire saying: IF YOU DON'T WANT TO TELL ME WHAT TIME YOU'RE COMING IN, I'LL SEE YOU AT THE HOTEL.

When I got Jack's next wire I knew he was getting a little irritated. It read: STOP FOOLING AROUND. I'M ARRIVING 10:30 SUNDAY MORNING. MEET ME AT THE STATION.

My next wire was: HOW COULD I MEET YOU, DIDN'T GET YOUR LAST WIRE.

Well, the next thing I knew I was deluged with telegrams from all over the country. Every one of them said JACK BENNY IS ARRIVING 10:30 SUNDAY MORNING, MEET HIM AT THE STATION. Jack had obviously gotten in touch with all of our friends and told them to send me these wires. I got telegrams from Sophie Tucker, Blossom Seeley, Benny Fields, Jay C. Flippen, Harry Richman, Al Jolson, Belle Baker, Eddie Cantor, George Jessel, Jesse Block, Eve Sully—I must have received about twenty-five wires. I pinned them all over the wall in my hotel room, and when Jack arrived, naturally I didn't meet him. He walked into my room about eleven o'clock and said, "George, why didn't you meet me?"

Very innocently I said, "I didn't know what time you were coming in."

Well, Jack looked at me, he looked at the wires, and then he fell on the bed laughing.

But there was one time when I saw Jack mad—and boy, was he mad. He had just finished playing nine holes of golf, and he came into the grill room and sat down at my table. I made the mistake of being nice, and said, "How's Mary?"

This seemed to set him off, and he practically shouted at me, "Don't ever mention Mary's name to me again!"

I said, "What happened?"

Angrily he said, "And don't ever mention Irving Fein's name again!"

"I didn't mention Irving Fein's name."

"Well, don't!"

"I won't."

"Good!"

"Well, what happened, Jack?"

He said, "Treating me like some kid just getting started in show business!"

"Jack," I said, "what did they do, those two people whose names I'm not supposed to mention?"

He didn't even hear me. "I've got half a notion to divorce Mary and fire Irving Fein," he muttered.

I said, "Jack, you've been married to Mary for thirty-eight years, and Irving Fein has been your manager for twenty-six years. Now, what is this horrible thing they both did?"

He said, "They insisted I sign an exclusive contract with NBC for three years! Who needs it? Why should I be tied up with one network for three years?"

I got the feeling there was more to this than just signing the contract, so I took a stab in the dark and said, "Jack, how was your golf game today?"

Slapping the table for emphasis, he said, "I played the worst game of golf I ever played in my life!"

Nothing further was said, but a few days later Jack came waltzing into the grill room like a ballerina.

I said, "Jack you look very happy, you must have shot a good game of golf."

He beamed all over. "I was fabulous. I had a forty-one for nine holes. It's the best golf I've played in years."

"You must be in a good mood," I said. "How do you feel about that three-year contract that Mary and Irving made you sign?"

"It's a marvelous contract! I'm lucky to have two wonderful people like Mary and Irving Fein looking out for me!" And he practically pirouetted out of the grill room. It's a good thing he didn't divorce Mary before he had that hot round of golf.

Before we were both married, Jack and I used to eat together almost every night. Now, eating with Jack was an experience I'll never forget. He never liked what he ordered, he only liked what you ordered. One night we were sitting in a restaurant, and he ordered a steak and I ordered roast beef. When our food came he looked at my roast beef and his mouth started to water. He said, "George, would you like a piece of my steak?"

I said, "No, then you'll want a piece of my roast beef."

Don't ask me why, but that struck him funny and he laughed so hard he fell off his chair twice.

The next night we were in the same restaurant and Jack said, "George, your roast beef looked so delicious last night I'm going to order it."

I said, "Good," and I ordered steak.

When our food came, he took a look at my steak and his mouth started to water. He said, "George, would you like a piece of my roast beef?"

I said, "No, because then you'll want a piece of my steak."

This time he only fell off the chair once because he'd heard that joke before.

Then the following night he ordered chicken and I had pot roast. He looked at my pot roast and his mouth started to water.

I said, "Hold it, you like pot roast?"

He said, "I love it," so I gave him my pot roast and took his chicken. He looked at my chicken and his mouth started to water. I got up and went to the men's room. It was making me nervous getting laughs with that kind of material. When I came back Jack wasn't there. I asked the waiter, "Did Mr. Benny leave?"

The waiter pointed and said, "No, he's right there under the table."

Now, you may think I'm exaggerating when I talk about Jack falling on the floor so often—but it's true. He'd collapse with laughter and literally fall on the floor. I don't know what his cleaning bill was, but it must have been tremendous.

I'm going to close this chapter with an anecdote about Jack Benny that you may have heard before, but I think it bears repeating. One day he went to his lawyer's office in Beverly Hills to sign a multi-million-dollar contract. I knew that it was a very big deal, so when Jack came into the club that afternoon I said to him, "Jack, you must be very excited."

"I certainly am," he said, "Do you know after I signed the contract I stopped at a little drugstore downstairs and, George, I finally found a place that serves a good cup of coffee!"

That was Jack Benny, my dearest and closest friend. And wherever Jack is I hope the coffee is good.

Live, Love and Enjoy It

When it comes to romance I'm at a very awkward age. If I go out with girls younger than me, I'm criticized. If I go out with girls older than me, I can't get them out of the rest home. But I look at it this way, I'd much rather be criticized than run around with some old kid that gets stoned on Lydia Pinkham cocktails.

My advice to any man my age is to go out with young girls—and my advice to any woman my age is to go out with young boys. But believe me, the important thing is that you go out. Don't just sit there watching game shows on television. However, if you enjoy watching television, at least do it with a young girl on your lap—that's for men. If you're a woman, have a young boy on your lap. Another thing, I think it's a good idea for couples like this to double-date. Then, about ten o'clock, when the old man and old woman get tired, the two kids can go out and enjoy themselves. Now, that's the creed I've lived by all my life, so you can see how mixed up I am.

But, on a more serious note, I should think that mothers would be tickled to death to have their daughters go out with me. After all, they meet interesting people, I take them to nice restaurants, we go to the theater . . . that's certainly better than riding around on the rear end of a motorcycle. Let's face it, I'm a very nice man to go out with. The only thing I expect from a girl is for her to light my cigar.

Now, it may come as a surprise to some people, but a lot

147

of these young girls I date would like to marry me. And why not? I've got a nice home in Beverly Hills with a swimming pool, two marvelous people working for me who keep the place looking like new, excellent food—all the comforts that any girl could wish for. Of course, I realize they don't want to marry me because I'm a sex symbol—I'm more of a security blanket.

It's a funny thing, but if I were their age, they wouldn't want to marry me at all. It's true, kids nowadays don't even think of getting married. If a boy and girl like each other, they live together. They have a couple of kids, the kids grow up, and if they like the looks of the kids, then they get married. And if it doesn't work out, they can always get a divorce, start living together, and be happy again.

I suppose you're all aware that nowadays anything goes. Everything is out in the open. Well, a perfect example is nudity. You go to the beaches and both men and women are sunbathing with nothing on. You can go to the theater and see a show where the entire cast is naked. And in the movies it's not uncommon to see men and women get into bed together naked. I guess that's all right for some people, but not for me. I even catch cold if I leave my house without wearing spats.

Wherever you go these days if it isn't complete nudity, it's the next thing to it. I flew in from New York recently and I had a script with me that I wanted to study on the flight. I figured those four and a half hours would be a perfect time to concentrate on learning my lines. However, I didn't even get the script open before I glanced up, and sitting opposite me was a young beautiful girl wearing a see-thru blouse. On me it was wasted. I've reached the point now where I forget what I'm supposed to look for.

That see-thru blouse made me very nervous. When I looked at it I sort of got the feeling it was looking back at me. In fact, over Albuquerque, I'm not sure but I think one of them winked at me. I not only didn't study my script, but when we landed I had trouble fastening my seat belt.

It's getting so that nothing shocks you anymore. But I remember a time when people were easily shocked. And the most shocking place of all was the burlesque theater. To be seen going in there was a disgrace. I used to go to the Olympic on 14th Street in New York City, and when I went in I'd hide my face and sit in the last row so nobody would see me. And it was quite a hassle, everybody was trying to sit in the last row. When the lights went up during intermission everybody always buried his head in a newspaper.

The big attraction then was a dancer who billed herself as "Gilda Goulay, the Girl with the American Beauty Rose." By today's standards her act was nothing, but we thought it was very wicked. It started with a loud drumroll, the houselights would go out, and a magenta spotlight would hit the stage. Then Gilda would make her entrance, and to the beat of the music she'd sensuously walk from one side of the stage to the other. She wore a black silk evening gown that clung to her body like it was painted on her. There was a slit up the front of the dress, and at the top of the slit she wore a big American Beauty rose. As Gilda paraded around, she did a series of little discreet bumps, and with each bump a single petal would fall off the rose. She had it timed so that when there was one lone petal left she made her exit. And that was her whole act. The audience went wild; they wanted her to drop that last petal. But Gilda wouldn't do that, she had too much class. She'd never stand in front of an audience with a naked stem. If any of you don't believe this story, you can check it with anybody—there was an Olympic theater on 14th Street. And if you want further proof, right across the street was Cornblatt's delicatessen store. Gilda used to eat there.

During that same era when Gilda was bumping her petals off, the average woman wore hobble skirts. These were long skirts that got very tight around the top of the shoe, and they had a slit on the side. When a woman would step up onto a streetcar, the slit would open and sometimes you could see five or six inches of her ankle. That was exciting. I

149

was twenty-two years old before I knew a woman's leg went higher than her ankle.

The favorite pastime for men in those days was to stand in front of the cigar store and watch women get onto street cars. And there was always some fresh, smartaleck wiseguy who'd whistle and holler, "Oh, you kid!" I hate myself for doing it now, but in looking back I realize that although I was only standing in front of a cigar store, I was trying to be a comedian even then. "Oh, you kid!" wasn't my only nifty remark. I had a snappy saying for every occasion. Like when I'd be dancing with a girl I'd say to her, "Honey, you're the bee's knees!" And if that didn't work, I'd hit her with my biggie, "Kid, you're the cat's pajamas!" That never missed.

Some of the other guys would use things like "23 Skid-doo!" "Ishkabibble!" or "Beat it!"—but not me. I left those corny ones for the amateurs. I had good stuff like "Make a noise like a hoop and roll away!"; "Lace up your shoe, your tongue is out!"; "Under the sink with the rest of the pipes!"; and "Turn over, your buckwheats are burning!" With comedy material like that, is it any wonder that I didn't have time for sex?

I know that today I have the reputation for being a sex kitten, but believe it or not, when I was seventeen or eighteen making out with girls didn't interest me. All I wanted to do was sing and dance and tell jokes. I was a great Peabody dancer (the Peabody came long before the Charleston and was tougher to do), and if I had a choice between two girls, one whom I knew I could make it with and the other I could enter a Peabody contest with and win a loving cup, the loving cup would win every time. I'd rather be on my toes than on my back. In those days I didn't bother with girls. The only thing I wanted to get into was show business.

There was one time when I got a crush on a little girl named Elsie McGrath. She was twelve years old, and I was thirteen—you see, I liked younger girls even then. Anyway, we used to go rollerskating in Hamilton Fish Park on

Sheriff Street, and I knew she was crazy about me because she used to let me hold her skate key.

Now, along about that time I read an article in the paper saying that the world's greatest tenor, Enrico Caruso, ate six cloves of garlic every day because he claimed it strengthened his vocal cords. Well, I loved to sing even then. I started when I was seven, and I always wanted to be a great singer, so I figured if six cloves of garlic was good enough for Caruso, it was good enough for me. I started eating six cloves of garlic a day, and believe me, this didn't help my popularity in the neighborhood. One day I played hooky from school and my mother got a thank-you note from my teacher.

I came from a big family, seven sisters and five brothers, and during my garlic period whenever I'd come into the house I'd get a standing ovation—they all not only got up but they left the room. But it did help my sleeping. I shared a small bed with my brother Sammy and my brother Willy. The minute I'd get into bed they'd go out the window and sleep on the fire escape and I had the whole bed to myself.

But my mother was smart. She knew how to take advantage of my pungent personality. Whenever a bill collector came to the door she'd have me answer it. I'd open the door and say, "What do you want?", and the guy would reel back, gasp, "Forget it!", and run down the hall.

However, it certainly did not help my romance with Elsie McGrath. Whenever I took her home I had to walk either in front of her or in back of her, depending on which way the wind was blowing. One afternoon when we reached her house she ran up to the top of her stoop, where I stopped her. "Elsie," I said, "this is the fourth time I've brought you home. Don't you think you should invite me in to meet your mother?"

Quickly she said, "You wait right there, George, and when I get upstairs I'll have my mother say hello to you from the window." And with that she bounded inside. In a couple of minutes the window opened and her mother looked out. I hollered up, "Hello, Mrs. McGrath!" and she slammed the window—and they lived on the fifth floor.

It finally got to the point where Elsie wouldn't walk on the same street with me, so I had to make a decision. It was either her skate key or singing like Caruso—and she had a very cute skate key. Just think, if it weren't for her cute skate key I might be singing at the Met and using Caruso's dressing room.

Years later, when Elsie was just a memory, I was still plugging along trying to make it in show business. I couldn't get a job and time was passing by. There I was, seventeen years old, but I wasn't ready to quit. I had some pretty goofy ideas in those days. I figured if I looked like an actor, somehow I'd get to be an actor. And boy, did I look like an actor. I borrowed some money from my brother-in-law and bought myself an outfit. It was a powder-blue suit with a white chalk-stripe, and the coat had five buttons down the front. With this I wore a double-breasted, pearl-gray vest with spats to match, and a high, starched collar with a snap-on polka-dot bow tie. And I topped it all off with a wide-brimmed straw hat that had a black string attached to my lapel. Also, I always had one cigar sticking out of my handkerchief pocket. I couldn't afford to smoke it, but I thought it made me look prosperous. That entire outfit cost me $12 not counting the cigar, which cost 7¢. When I put it on, it changed my whole personality. I even walked differently. I sort of bounced when I walked so that people would know I was a dancer, too. And I always had a self-satisfied grin on my face. I thought I looked absolutely marvelous and it seemed everybody else thought so, too, because people kept staring at me.

And since I was looking like an actor I had to act like one. Now, at that time Hammerstein's Theater on 42nd Street and Broadway was the most outstanding vaudeville theater in the world. All the actors used to congregate in front of it. I reasoned if I mingled with this crowd, some agent or producer might notice me and give me a job. I had all kinds of classy theatrical poses which I thought would attract their attention. Sometimes I would only button the top button of my five-button coat so I could flare back the bottom and put one hand in my pants pocket with my thumb sticking out and my feet spread apart. Other times I'd flare back both sides of my coat and put both hands in my pants pocket with my thumbs sticking out. Then again I might hook both thumbs in my vest pocket, or hold on to both lapels, or I might even lean casually against the building with my legs crossed and gracefully hold my unlit cigar in my hand. I didn't do that one too often because I didn't want the cigar to unravel.

Anyway, producers passed, agents passed, and they always looked at me but they never offered me a job. But that didn't bother me; I felt that being out of work was part of show business.

Show business even influenced the type of girl I went out with. If I took a girl on a date, she had to be a great ballroom dancer, and wear rouge and lipstick and beaded eyelashes. That was my idea of what an actress should look like. And if she wore a beauty mark, I'd even let her stand with me in front of Hammerstein's.

With me being out of work, I suppose you're wondering how I could afford to take a girl out on a date. Well, you must remember that taking a girl out then was a lot different than it is today. In the first place, the girl didn't even expect you to take her to dinner. You'd just say, "Meet me at eight o'clock in front of Webster Hall." There was always a dance at Webster Hall, and the admission was 25¢ for women and 35¢ for men. Then, after dancing for about two hours, the two of you would have a root beer—that was another 10¢. After the dance you'd spend a dime taking the subway to Chinatown where you'd split a bowl of chow mein for 40¢, and leave a 10¢ tip for the waiter. Then you'd take the subway, which was another dime. The entire evening would cost you $1.40, and the girl let you kiss her goodnight because you'd been such a big sport.

153

A night on the town for $1.40—nowadays it costs you more than that just to park your car. The other night I had a date with a girl and we had dinner at a nice restaurant, went to see a show, had a couple of drinks after the show, and it cost me $82. And when she drove me home she wouldn't let me kiss her goodnight. She didn't want me to smear her makeup because after she left me she had a late date with somebody else.

Women today are very independent. All you hear about is Women's Liberation and the role they want to assume in modern society. They want to do the same work men do and get paid the same money for doing it. And I'm all for it. Last week I went out with a pretty young girl, and she was a plumber. It cost me another $82 and she couldn't do a damned thing for my pipes.

One of the big issues in Women's Lib is that they want to get out of the kitchen. My mother never would have gone along with this. There were twelve kids in my family, and my mother's idea of liberation was to get into the kitchen. She'd do anything to get out of that bedroom.

Now, just because there were twelve kids in my family didn't mean that my father was a great lover. It meant that we were very poor. We couldn't afford any coal or wood, and in the wintertime it was freezing in our house. When you get into bed and you're that cold, anybody can be a great lover. If we had lived in California, I might have been an only child.

Well, I don't know if this chapter has done anything to help your love life, but if it's given you a few laughs, I'm satisfied. But one last thought—no matter what age you are, live, love, and enjoy it!

To Write a Book You Need a Sharp Pencil

Since you've read this far into the book, I assume you must be very interested—or one of my relatives. Either way I'm going to tell you how this whole thing happened. One morning I was sitting in my office at General Service Studio with my writer, Elon Packard, and my secretary, Jack Langdon. We were in the middle of writing a silly letter to an old vaudeville friend of mine, Jesse Block, when the door burst open and in came Irving Fein, who by now was my personal manager. He was all excited and said, "George, I've got marvelous news! I just got a firm offer for you to write a book for Putnam's. What do you think of that?"

I said, "Not now, Irving, I'm in the middle of writing a letter to Jesse Block."

"But, George—" Irving stammered.

I said, "Please, Irving, this is important."

Well, a very deflated Irving Fein sat down on the couch while we finished that cockamamie letter. Then, very deliberately, I fixed myself a cup of tea, lit a cigar, crossed my legs and, turning to Irving, said in my most studied and casual delivery, "Now, Irving, what is it you wanted to talk about?"

"Two can play at this game, George," Irving said, and he deliberately got up and fixed himself a cup of tea.

Well, we finally got down to business, and Irving repeated what he'd said before about Putnam's wanting me to write a book.

I said, "Well, Irving, they came to the right guy. If I can

write a letter to Jesse Block, I can certainly knock out a book."

Irving put down his cup of tea and said, "Okay, George, we've both had our little fun this morning, now let's get serious. What do you think of the idea?"

I said, "Irving, I think it's a sensational idea and I'll definitely do it—but first let me think about it."

Well, that did it for Irving. He got up from the couch and headed for the door. I had to grab him by the arm to keep him from leaving. "Irving, I'm sorry," I said. "Of course I'll do it." He then told me the details, the next day I signed the contract, and that's how the deal was made.

I had written a book before back in 1955. It was called *I Love Her, That's Why!*, and I did it in collaboration with a writer named Cynthia Hobard Lindsay. She was a charming young lady and a top-notch writer. We used to meet at my house on weekends and I'd talk to her while she made notes. Then, during the week, she'd put it together. Cynthia did a very fine job, and it turned out to be a good book.

However, this time I wanted to be more personally involved with the actual writing, which I have been from the very first page. Now, I'm not the kind of a guy who can sit down at a typewriter or get a pad and pencil and start writing a book. In the first place, I never got any applause for my spelling. I spell "cat" with a capital *k* and two *t*'s. So I decided the only logical thing to do was to write the book the same way I put my comedy routines together. And that's the way it's being written. Every morning I come into my office and meet with Elon Packard, whom we call Packy, and Jack Langdon, whom we call Jack Langdon—we couldn't think of anything else to call him.

Now let me tell you how the three of us work together. Each one of us has his own particular function, and I think I'll start with me. Why not, it's my book. To begin with, in the true sense of the word I am not a writer. But I do have a good comedy mind; I think funny and I say things funny.

When Gracie and I first started to move up in show business we made eight two-reel shorts for Warner Bros. and Paramount. Each film ran nine or ten minutes, and I put them together all alone without any writers. The success of these films did a lot for our careers.

Later on, when we got into radio and television, we were able to hire writers, but I always worked right along with them. I seemed to have an instinct for what would make people laugh.

One of the most important things for a performer to learn is timing. The same thing applies to writing a comedy sketch, or a nightclub routine, or an after-dinner speech, or even to writing this book. The writing should have a rhythm to it so the reader feels he is actually listening to the words. Now that I've explained what I do, I'd appreciate it if one of you readers would write in and explain it to me.

Now let me get to the other two guys in the room. Packy has been with me for twelve years. When he was eighteen he started writing in radio for Milton Berle, and since then he has written for most of the top comics in the business. For the past eight years Packy has been with me exclusively, but only for two hours a day. When twelve o'clock comes he's on his own, and he frequently writes for his long-time friend George Gobel, and any other assignments that come up. Packy is a very funny writer, and I personally like him because he's able to phrase words in a way that fit my mouth. My only problem was breaking him of the habit of writing words with more than two syllables, because I have a very small mouth.

Anyway, Packy has a lot of free time, and if any of you readers have to make a speech at an Elk's Club, or a bar mitzvah, or even if you want to say something funny to your wife, get in touch with Packy. He can be found most afternoons at the bar of the Tail o' the Cock on Ventura Boulevard. He does some of his funniest writing on bar napkins.

Now to Jack Langdon. He's been with me for sixteen

years, and his is a full-time job. He runs my office, he makes sure all my bills are paid, he handles my correspondence, he coordinates all my activities—but his most important job, what you might consider his chief duty, is to make sure I don't make a date with two girls on the same night. He's a pretty shrewd kid. He's arranged things so it would be absolutely impossible for me to get rid of him. He's figured out a filing system of all my comedy routines, monologues, and songs, which is so damned complicated that when he puts something away he's the only one who knows where it is. I don't think even the CIA could break his code. If Jack ever leaves me, I'm back to being a straight man again.

Now, in the room when we're writing, Jack sits at the typewriter and he's sort of our balance wheel. Sometimes Packy and I will get hold of a funny idea and we'll work on it, kick it around, play with it and develop it until it becomes a funny little routine—and we always make sure the wording is just the way we want it. Then we're ready to tell it to Jack—and we do. But Jack isn't always ready to write it down. He just sits there stubbornly staring at the typewriter. Well, after a moment I lean toward Packy and say, "Packy, I get a feeling that Jack doesn't think our routine is funny."

Packy looks at me and says, "Why don't we ask him?"

"Well," I say, "do you want to ask him, or should I?"

Packy answers, "You better ask him. You're sitting closer to him."

"All right, I'll ask him." I turn to Jack and say, "Jack, why don't you think our routine is funny?"

Jack looks right at me and says, "All right, you and Packy have your fun, but all you do is sit there and write one joke after another. When you're writing a book you have to paint a word picture. Who are these people? How are they dressed? Where did they come from—where are they going? Are they happy—are they sad?"

Letting what he just said sink in, and being a reasonable man, I say, "Jack, I happen to think that little routine Packy

158

and I just finished is terribly funny, and I don't want to clutter it up with where the people have been or where they're going."

His voice rising, Jack sputters, "But, George, it's important for the readers to know these things!"

Then in a very quiet voice I say, "Jack, you've made a good point, and I respect your opinion. And you certainly have the right to express yourself. But before you go any further, just stop and think—who is it that signs your paycheck every Friday?"

After a split-second pause, Jack says, "Fellows, I was wrong. I think it's a very, very funny routine. Now tell it to me again so I can write it down." By now Packy and I have forgotten the routine, and Jack has won again—I told you he was a shrewd kid.

If people knew some of the things that go on in this office, they'd back up a wagon and take us away. A while back I came into the office and said, "Jack, will you do me a favor? I'm running low on jockey shorts, can you pick me up a dozen pair?"

Jack said, "Sure, what kind do you wear?"

So I took down my pants and showed him. Well, Jack took a look and said, "Why don't you get the same kind that I wear?"

"What kind do you wear?" I said, and Jack took down his pants. There we stood, two full-grown men with our pants down, comparing jockey shorts. Well, just at that moment the door opened and in walked Packy. He took one look at us and said, "I suppose you fellows want to be alone," and walked out. Jack pulled up his pants, ran out, and brought Packy back, and we went to work on the book. It was kind of a hot day so I just sat there in my jockey shorts.

But I don't want you to get the idea that things like that happen every day—they don't. They happen four times a day. Naturally, we have our differences and our arguments, but when the air clears we always manage to get it down on paper. Packy and Jack don't even think of me as the boss.

159

That's because I'm the easiest person in the world to get along with—as long as they agree with me.

Well, now that I've explained our little group I suppose you're wondering how we ever get anything done. I don't know either, but somehow we do.

Now, right here I'd like to clear up something. Lots of people have the idea that all of these anecdotes and stories I tell are a bunch of lies. I resent that. I don't deny it, but I resent it. What I'm trying to say is that everything you'll read in this book actually happened. Oh, when we work on a story we might bend it a little, give it a new beginning, make the end a little funnier—but the middle is always—or maybe it's the beginning—or sometimes it's the end—but at least part of every story is based on truth! And I'm not sure of that, either.

The Peewee Quartet. George is on the left.

George and one of his first partners in vaudeville, Bill Lorraine.

George doing a seal act in early vaudeville.

Gracie, sitting on the pedestal with her sisters Pearl, Bessie, and Hazel. In San Francisco.

Gracie at sixteen.

Left to right: George, Gracie, Eddie Cantor, George Jessel, Janet Reed. Backstage at The Palace. *Photo by White Studio.*

George and Gracie on their first trip to Europe in 1928.

Gracie with Senator Alben W. Barkley (later he became Vice President), during the radio days.

The family, when Ronnie and Sandy were very small.
Photo by Tom Kelley.

Left to right: Gracie, Fred Clark, Bea Benadaret and George, in a scene from a Burns and Allen TV show.

Portrait of Gracie Allen. *Photo by John Engstead.*

Gracie, Isabel Jewell, and George in a classic moment from the Burns and Allen TV show.

The family, when Ronnie and Sandy were teenagers.

George and Gracie in front of their home in Beverly Hills.

Left to right: Ronald Reagan, Gracie, James Cagney, Danny Thomas at testimonial dinner for Burns and Allen.

George and Gracie at a festive dinner in 1950.

George and Gracie during the Burns and Allen TV days.

Left to right: William Paley, Gracie, and Sam Goldwyn.

Left to right: Gracie, Danny Kaye, George Jessel, and George, at a Friars testimonial dinner for George and Gracie in 1955. *CBS photo by Gabor Rona.*

Jack Benny, Gracie, and George in one of those gag photographs. *Photo by Gene Lester.*

Left to right: Jack and Mary Benny, George and Gracie, relaxing at a rehearsal for a benefit show.

George with Jack Benny doing an impersonation of Gracie. *Photo by Eddie Hoff.*

Robert Young, Eleanor Powell, Gracie and George, in the MGM movie *Honolulu.*

Gracie, W. C. Fields, Mary Boland, and George in a scene from the Paramount picture *Six of a Kind.*

Judy Garland, Carol Channing, and George in Las Vegas.

George and Carol Channing working together in a theater engagement.

Left to right: Larry Keating, Harry Von Zell, and George having fun on the Burns and Allen TV series.

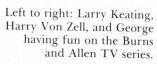

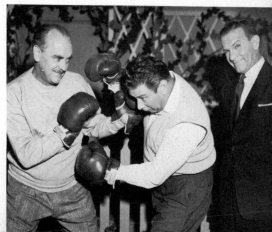

Left to right: George Jessel, George Burns, Eddie Cantor, and Jack Benny harmonizing on a TV special for NBC. *NBC photo by Elmer Holloway.*

Jack Benny and George on a vacation in Hawaii.

Bing Crosby, George, and Jack Benny on the Burns and Allen TV show.

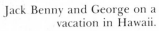

Jack Benny, George Jessel, George Burns, and Al Jolson at a Friars affair.

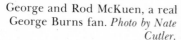

George and Rod McKuen, a real George Burns fan. *Photo by Nate Cutler.*

George and his personal manager, Irving Fein. *Photo by Nate Cutler.*

George with Arlette and Daniel D'Hoore. They keep everything running smoothly at his home in Beverly Hills. *Photo by Nate Cutler.*

George receives proclamation from Los Angeles Mayor Tom Bradley citing him as "The New Star of 1976" by the Variety Club of Southern California.

George, with Ann-Margret and Carol Channing, backstage in Las Vegas. *Photo by Las Vegas News Bureau.*

George and Lisa Miller, still
singing "The Maple Leaf Rag"?
Photo by Nate Cutler.

George and Joanna Baer. *Photo by
Peter C. Borsari.*

George at the National Association
of Theater Owners convention in
New Orleans with his "Star of
Tomorrow" award and two
attractive presenters.

Ann-Margret and George singing one of George's big hits. *Photo by Julian Wasser,* Time *Magazine.*

George and Lita Baron arriving at a charity premiere. *Photo by Tom McEnery.*

George, Walter Matthau, and Richard Benjamin in the MGM picture *The Sunshine Boys.*

Left to right: Herb Ross, Walter Matthau, George, and Neil Simon rehearsing *The Sunshine Boys* at MGM.

George and his "Oscar" for Best Supporting Actor of 1975. *Photo by Long Photography.*

Walter Matthau and George at a college press conference in New York City. *Photo by Paul Schumach, Metropolitan Photo Service.*

Left to right: Elon Packard, Jack Langdon, and George, working on the book at the office. *Photo by Nate Cutler.*

George, Big Ben, and Walter Matthau in London for the opening of *The Sunshine Boys.*

It's Easy To Ad-lib If You've Got It Written Down

I guess by now you've got the idea that I'm in love with show business. I don't know what line of business you're in—whether you're a banker, a druggist, a used car dealer, or run a taco stand—but whatever you do, my advice would be to quit right now and get into show business. The reason I make this suggestion is that it worked for me, and for a very long time. Of course, maybe you're not cut out for show business; maybe you can't sing, or dance, or act, or be funny, but don't let that worry you—I made it.

What I'm trying to say is, whatever line of work you get into, or whatever you do, make sure it's something you love, something you enjoy doing. To my way of thinking, if you can accomplish this, you're bound to be successful. And I'm talking from experience. I fell in love with show business when I was seven years old, and for years and years and years things were very tough for me and I got very few jobs. But that didn't stop me, I'd much rather be a flop in show business than a success making felt hats. It's a damned good thing I didn't go into felt hats because they're not wearing them anymore.

To give you an idea of how much being in the theater meant to me, even when I was very young and laying off I never let anybody know it. I used to ride up and down in the elevator of the Putnam Building where all the agents had offices. I'd have makeup on the top of my collar, my music under one arm and my pictures under the other. If an agent saw me, I wanted him to know I was ready. One day, after riding up and down six or seven times, the elevator boy said to me, "I know you're an actor, but do you play anyplace besides this elevator?"

In those days I'd do anything to further my feeble career. Here's an example: When I was about nineteen I knew an actor named Willie Delight, who had two thousand cards printed which read, *Willie Delight, Songs, Dances & Syncopated Patter.* Well, after he'd used about eighty of the cards he decided to go into some other business. I couldn't pass up an opportunity like that, so I bought 1,920 cards for $2, and changed my name to Willie Delight. After I used up all the cards I went back to my old name—Harry Pierce. That was a lucky name for me—I once got a job to play a Sunday concert in Ronkonkoma with it.

But through the years show business has been good to me, and it's given me a very exciting life. It's not just the spotlight, the music, the laughter, the applause, the fame, the— Not true! It *is* the spotlight, the music, the laughter, the applause, and the fame. But besides all that you meet some of the most interesting people in the world. Now, most of these people work behind the scenes. There are producers, agents, directors, stagehands, choreographers, theater managers—but there's one breed of characters that stands out from all the rest: comedy writers. Believe me I know, because as I said I've worked closely with comedy writers for the last forty-five years. I always tried to hire the best because I know how important the words are when you face an audience.

To be a good comedy writer you should have a basic intelligence, a good sense of humor, a flare for phrasing, a feeling for current comedy trends, and an understanding of human nature. Now, all comedy writers may not have every one of these qualities, but there is one characteristic that is an absolute must—they've got to be on the nutty side. By that I don't mean that they're candidates for the booby hatch, but they all have little peculiarities and idiosyncracies that the average person doesn't have. I can say this because I'm a little on the nutty side myself.

I couldn't possibly tell you about all the writers who worked for me over the years. My memory isn't what it used to be, there's a paper shortage, and I don't want to be late for my bridge game, so I'll just mention a few incidents to give you an idea of what I'm talking about.

As long as I've already mentioned Packy, I'll start with him. Back when he first started writing, he thought he should get himself some sort of identity, so he got a bright idea and decided to wear nothing but red socks. He figured if a producer couldn't remember his name, he'd say, "Why don't we hire that kid who wears red socks?" So that's all Packy ever wore. No matter what kind of an outfit he had on, or what color it was, he always wore his red socks. However, it backfired on him. He was up for a job one time and he was turned down. Later he found out the reason why—the producer had said, "I'd never hire that kid, he never changes his socks." Personally I'm glad he still wears red socks, because sometimes I can't remember his name.

Back in the early days of radio there was a writer named Harry Conn, who not only worked for me, but also worked for Jack Benny. He was with me about four or five months, but he did certain things that I couldn't take. He went on to work exclusively with Jack and did a great job because he was a fine writer—but he was not for me. One of the things I couldn't take was his colossal ego. He'd come in with three of four pages of jokes, then he'd tear off one joke and give it to me to read. After I read it he'd tear off another joke and give that to me. Well, the first time he did this, I said to him, "Harry, what is it with this tearing bit? Why don't you just give me the four pages and let me read them?"

He said, "George, I want my jokes to be appreciated. I write them one at a time, and I want you to read them one at a time. It's like fine wine—you don't gulp it down, you sip it." After he hit me with that last line I had the feeling that Harry Conn was soon going to be drinking alone.

163

Anyway, the way we worked there were three of us in the room. Besides Harry Conn and myself there was Carroll Carroll, a writer who was hired by the J. Walter Thompson Agency. But this setup didn't agree with Harry because he thought he could do everything by himself. One day while Carroll was out of the room, and after Harry had torn off two pages of jokes, he said, "George, I can't work with another writer in the room. Either you get rid of Carroll or you get rid of me."

Well, I just sat there with my hands full of this funny confetti he had just handed me. "Harry," I said, "I happen to think Carroll Carroll is a fine writer, but that's beside the point. Carroll Carroll is paid by J. Walter Thompson—I am paid by J. Walter Thompson—you are paid by me. So I can't fire Carroll Carroll. In fact, I think Carroll Carroll might be able to fire me. So, Harry, why don't you take a walk around the block, think about it and cool off. And if you still want me to fire Carroll Carroll, just keep walking."

Harry left, slamming the door behind him. Ten minutes later he was back, tore off another joke, and we all went back to work again.

Now let me tell you what ended our relationship. This particular morning he came in, tore off his first joke, and gave it to me.

I read it, tore it up, and said, "I don't like it."

He was indignant. "What do you mean you don't like it?"

I said, "It's not funny. Your fine wine has fermented."

"George," Harry snapped back, "if you don't like that joke, you know nothing about comedy. If you lock me in a room with George S. Kaufman and Moss Hart, I guarantee you I'll write funnier stuff than they do!"

I said, "I'm sorry to hear that, Harry. George S. Kaufman and Moss Hart are very expensive writers. Now, if your stuff is better than theirs, you might as well leave because you deserve a lot more money than I can afford to pay." With that I opened the door and said, "Good-bye, Harry!"

So Harry left. After he was gone I glued the pieces of that

164

joke together, and Gracie and I did it on the air. It didn't get a laugh. Harry was wrong, I do know something about comedy.

Another writer who worked with me during that same period was John P. Medbury. To me, Medbury never looked like a writer. Come to think of it, none of my writers ever looked like writers. In fact, I don't know what a writer is supposed to look like, but they can certainly look better than they do. I think I look more like a writer than my writers did. I wear expensive clothes, I always have a silk scarf tied around my neck, I always carry a couple of ballpoint pens along with a little notebook pad, and when I come to the office I always wear my suede jacket with the leather patches on the elbows. But there's one problem—I can't write.

Anyway, Medbury was about 5'5" or 5'6", and must have weighed 250 pounds. He was not only a writer, but he was a big eater. And he looked more like an eater than a writer. But even though he was one of the best writers I ever had, he never laughed at anything, not even his own stuff. He never changed his stone-faced expression. It wasn't that he didn't have a marvelous sense of humor, it was just that he knew practically every joke that was ever written. So if you tried to tell him a joke, before you got the first line out of your mouth he'd tell you the punch line.

Even when he wasn't working at it he always had a quick dry wit, and he was never stuck for an answer. I remember one time standing with him on the corner of Hollywood Boulevard and Vine Street, and a strange man came up to him and asked, "Can I get to Sunset Boulevard this way?"

Without batting an eye, Medbury answered, "Yes, but only this once!" That was about twenty-five years ago and I'll bet that man is still standing there trying to figure out what Medbury meant.

At that time Medbury had an office in the Hollywood Plaza Hotel and was writing two syndicated humor columns for the newspapers. One was called "Mr. & Mrs." and the other was called "Mutter and Mumble." He hired a young fellow named Frank Williams to work for him. Frank was an ambitious young fellow trying to get started as a writer.

Now, right here I think I should explain that from time to time Medbury would entertain certain young ladies in his office. Well, one day Mrs. Medbury happened to drop in, and while looking for a stamp she opened the top drawer of Medbury's desk, and there was a pair of black lace panties. Gingerly holding them up, she looked at Medbury and said coldly, "John, what are these doing here?"

Again, without batting an eye Medbury angrily called into the other office, "Frank, get in here!"

The bewildered young writer walked in, and Medbury threw the panties at him, saying, "Give these back to your girl. You're fired!"

On her way out, Mrs. Medbury stopped at Frank's desk and said, "Frank, you're not fired. And tell lover-boy it didn't work. He's not as fast as he used to be."

Now, earlier in this chapter I stated that comedy writers are a little on the nutty side. And if this next story doesn't prove my point, nothing will. When this incident took place I was in radio and Medbury was my head writer. By now he had his offices on Gower Street, right next to Columbia Pictures, and every year I had to go there to negotiate a new contract with him. And it wasn't easy.

His outer office was a comfortable room with several chairs, a couch, and a well-stocked bar. Behind the bar were a number of shelves filled with all sorts of canned exotic foods. He had things like rattlesnake meat, chocolate-coated bumblebees, and fried grasshoppers. I remember one year at contract time I walked into his office, and after he fixed me a drink he said, "George, I just made myself a kangaroo sandwich and it's really delicious. Would you like one?"

I said, "No thanks, John, it would ruin my appetite. For dinner Gracie's fixing me some sautéed antelope ears."

Well, now it was time to talk business, so we took our

166

drinks and went into the other office where Medbury did his writing. In there was a large desk with a swivel chair behind it, and on the desk were four containers full of sharpened pencils. Medbury wrote everything in longhand. Over in one corner of the room was a table with four chairs.

Now get a good grip on the book. Seated in one of the chairs was a life-sized dummy of an American Indian in full regalia. This didn't shock me because it happened every year. The Indian was part of a little game Medbury played whenever he would sign a contract. I never did figure out whether Medbury was serious or not, but I played right along with him because I had to. He was my top writer and I didn't want to lose him.

Here's the way it went: We sat down at the table with the Indian, and Medbury said, "George, you remember the Chief."

"Of course," I said. Then, turning to the Chief, "Nice seeing you again, Chief. I notice you got a new headdress."

Medbury said, "That's not new, that's the same one he had last year."

I said, "Oh, I'm sorry, Chief, it looked new to me." Then I tried to get down to business. "John, it's contract time again. How about signing for next season?"

Medbury took a sip of his drink, then said, "George, we'll do it the same way we did it last year. You know I don't make a move unless the Chief okays it. So you better explain the deal to him."

I took a swallow of my drink and said, "Chief, it's very simple. You know, John has been with me for four years now, and every year I give him a hundred-dollar raise . . . and I'd like to do the same thing this year. It's been a very good relationship, and you okayed it last year, and I'm sure you will again."

"George," Medbury said, "you're coming on a little strong. Don't put words in the Chief's mouth. Give him time to think this out himself."

So we just sat there. After I finished my drink I said,

"John, the Chief's been thinking now for about ten minutes. When is he going to come up with an answer?"

Getting up from the table, Medbury said softly, "George, the Chief's in one of his quiet moods. You better leave now before you louse up the deal."

I whispered back, "Well, when can I expect his decision?"

Medbury said, "I'll talk it over with him and call you in the morning."

With that the meeting was over and I tiptoed out. The last thing I wanted was an Apache mad at me. As soon as I left there I got into my car and drove straight home to see Gracie. I wanted to talk to somebody who made a little sense. But the next morning Medbury called up and said, "George, the Chief slept on it and he's okayed the deal," and he hung up.

At that time Gracie and I were in the Top Ten of all the shows on radio, and here we were at the mercy of a stuffed Indian!

One thing I learned in my long association with comedy writers is that they come from all walks of life. I knew one writer who started out as a taxi driver; another was a tailor; then there was a policeman and a carpenter; I even hired one who was a cutter of ladies' dresses. One night some friends brought a young priest over for dinner. He was a very funny fellow and had us screaming all night long. After dinner I said to him, "Father, you've got a terrific sense of humor. Now, I don't know if you're allowed to do it or not, but we could certainly use a writer like you on our television show. In your spare time would you like to work for us?"

He gave me a benevolent smile and said, "That's a very flattering offer, George, but I don't think I could get away with moonlighting—I've got a very sharp Boss."

But there was one writer I discovered accidentally. He started out working for his father as a jewelry salesman. Gracie and I were playing Shea's theater in Buffalo, and one day before the matinee a young man came into my dressing room. He was a tall, gangling fellow with big feet and stooped shoulders. He said his name was Al Boasberg and asked if I would like to buy some jewelry. He opened his sample case, and as I was looking at the jewelry he started telling me jokes he'd written. And they were darned funny. After I heard a few I closed the case and said to him, "Did you really write this stuff yourself?"

He said, "Yeah."

"Well, then, you're in the wrong business," I said. "You ought to be a writer."

With that we started talking, and in the course of the conversation I got an idea. I knew a very old joke that I was crazy about. I had always wanted to use it in our act, but I couldn't figure out a way to switch it to make it sound new. I thought this would be a good chance to test this kid and see if he could really write. So I said to Boasberg, "See if you can switch this joke," and I told it to him.

I had no sooner gotten it out of my mouth than another comedy team, Harris & Pilsner, came into my dressing room. Well, I wanted to make Al Boasberg feel good, so I introduced him as a bright new comedy writer. Harris' face lit up, and he said to Boasberg, "Boy, can we use you! There's a hole right in the middle of our act where we need one good joke. If you can come up with one we can use, I'll give you fifty bucks for it."

What do you think Al Boasberg did? Without even looking at me he told Harris & Pilsner that same old joke that I had just told him. Well, they loved it, bought it, gave him $50, and left the dressing room on cloud nine.

I just sat there staring at Boasberg. "Kid," I said, "you've got a big future as a writer. You've not only got a great sense of humor, but you already learned how to steal!"

Boasberg grinned at me and put the $50 in his pocket.

I continued, "Now, Boasberg, I'd like to get serious with you. I've been in this business for a long time, and, kid, that's not the way to start. If you want to really succeed, one—you have to be original; two—you have to be honest; and three—you owe me twenty-five dollars!"

Anyway, three weeks later I brought Al Boasberg to New York and he went on to become one of the top comedy writers in the business. Besides Gracie and myself he worked for Jack Benny, Buster Keaton, the Marx Brothers, and many others. Now, as far as writing went, Boasey wouldn't sit down at a typewriter and put together a script. But if somebody else wrote the script, you'd give it to Boasey and he'd punch it up for you. He was sort of a doctor of comedy, and he was great at it. His lines always made the script funnier.

Boasey looked at the funny side of everything, and he loved practical jokes. I remember right after he got married, he was living here in California, but he'd never met his wife's folks. Well, her parents planned a trip out here to meet their new son-in-law, and the day they arrived Boasey's wife asked him to meet them at the airport while she prepared a nice meal for them. This started the wheels turning in Boasey's head. At that time Boasey was driving a big, black Cadillac, and on the way to the airport he stopped off at Western Costume Company and rented a chauffeur's outfit. When he got to the airport and met his wife's parents he was a picture of the perfect high-class chauffeur. He put their luggage into the trunk, helped them into the back seat, made sure they were comfortable, etc. They were very much impressed.

While driving home the mother said to Boasey, "I really didn't expect a chauffeur-driven car. My daughter's husband must be doing very well."

Playing it straight, Boasey said, "Oh, yes, he's probably the best comedy writer in Hollywood."

"Well, I've never met him," the mother continued. "What kind of a man is he?"

Boasberg answered, "He's probably the finest man I ever met in my entire life." Then, "Maybe I shouldn't say this, but it's a shame what his wife is doing to him behind his back!"

In a shocked voice, the mother gasped, "What on earth is she doing to him?"

"Well, for one thing she started sleeping with me even before she got married," Boasberg stated.

The rest of the trip was in absolute silence. When Boasey pulled the car into the driveway, his wife came out the front door to greet them, and as the stunned parents looked on, he grabbed her in his arms, spun her around, patted her fanny, and gave her a great big kiss. Then he said, "Honey, your folks are here."

As soon as his wife saw the chauffeur's uniform she knew he was up to one of his practical jokes. She patiently explained to her confused parents that Boasey was her husband, and after everything was straightened out they all had a good laugh—that is, everybody except the mother. She never did really warm up to Boasberg.

Although Boasey was a master of the practical joke, there was a time when one of them backfired. One of his best friends was another writer named Andy Douglas. One day Boasey went to visit Andy and when he arrived at the house he found a bicycle on the front porch. Well, Boasey couldn't pass that up. He took off his pants, opened the front door, and rode the bicycle into the living room in his shorts. There were about twelve people sitting there, and Boasey kept circling around the room on the bicycle. When he noticed that nobody was laughing, he stopped circling and said, "What's wrong with you people? You act like somebody died."

Andy said, "Somebody did—my mother. She's in the next room." Boasey peddled out the front door, and I don't think he pulled another practical joke for about two days.

The writers I've spoken about up to this point worked for me in vaudeville and radio. Later on, when I became involved in television, I remember hiring a team of very good writers named Seaman Jacobs and F-F-F-Fred F-F-F-Fox. The reason I wrote it that way is that Freddie stuttered. I don't mind telling a few stories about Freddie's stuttering because he never stops making jokes about it himself. On the other hand, his partner, Seaman Jacobs, whom we always call Si, is a very articulate, well-spoken man. What didn't make any sense was when they came into a meeting Freddie did all the talking and Si just sat there.

Now, when we used to put a script together the first step was for Freddie and Si to come in with a story line and read it to me. If I liked it, then it would be developed further into a complete script. A story line could sometimes be as long as five or six pages, and who do you think read it to me—F-F-Freddie. And the way Freddie told a story line, it took a l-l-l-long time. When Freddie started reading a story line I'd never stop him, because it took him an hour to get s-s-s-started. But it was worth it; they were always good and the scripts turned out funny.

Once when I was alone with Si I asked him, "Si, you could read that story line in one-tenth the time it takes Freddie. Why do you have him do it?"

Si said, "George, the way Freddie talks he needs all the practice he can get."

Well, I couldn't argue with that, so every Monday morning Freddie would come in and read the story line. One morning he was going along as usual when he came to a scene that he got very enthused about. In his excitement he read through the entire scene without once stuttering. When he was finished I said, "Freddie, do you realize that you just read three pages without stuttering?"

Freddie's eyes widened, and he jumped up, shouting, "My God, I'm c-c-c-cured!"

During this time there was another writer working for me, and the other fellows found out he was part Polish. Well, naturally they made him the butt of all those Polish jokes that were going around. He put up with it for a while, then one day he said to Freddie, "I wish the guys would stop hitting me with those lousy Polish jokes."

Freddie said, "Well, it's your own f-f-f-fault. You shouldn't have told them you were p-p-p-part Polish. Just like I shouldn't have t-t-t-told them I st-st-st-stutter."

The season was going along smoothly, and then one day Freddie had to go to the doctor. So on that Monday morning Si came in and read the story line. What usually took Freddie two hours took Si ten minutes. Well, I was so used to hearing Freddie's delivery that the whole thing fell flat. I said, "Si, I don't like this story line. You guys better come up with another one."

The next morning they came back and Freddie took two hours to read me that same story line, and I loved it. Si just shook his head and said, "George, that does it. If I want to stay in this business, I better learn how to st-st-st-stutter."

Now, before I lock up this section on Si and Freddie, I must tell you one quick little line that Freddie hit me with once. As he left the office he said, "G-G-G-George, if you have a p-p-p-problem with the script, just c-c-c-call my house. If nobody answers, th-th-th-that's me."

Anyway, Seaman and Freddie are still together, and I'm sure they'll never split up, because neither of them could ever find a nicer partner to work with.

Of all the writers I've worked with I've yet to find two with the exact same temperament. Some are easy going, some are excitable, some work fast, some work slow, some work alone, some need a partner, and some work best just kicking jokes around in a room with other writers.

At one time my writers would bring in four or five pages each morning, and each writer would take his turn reading his own material. This created a problem for me to decide what was funny or not. You see, some writers had a great delivery and made everything sound funny, while others were more introverted and just mumbled their words. I found myself being sold on stuff that wasn't funny and not using stuff that was. However, I finally solved the problem; I let my secretary, Jack Langdon, read everybody's material. That way everybody got a fair shake because Jack had no delivery at all.

Let me quickly give you an idea of how bad Jack's delivery was. When I did the television series "Wendy and Me" with Connie Stevens, I'd have Jack read Connie's part when I auditioned other actors. His readings were so awful that I almost got rid of Connie and hired another actress. (I hope that last anecdote gets into the book, because Jack is typing this stuff.)

You know, when you're working with four or five writers sitting in a room things do not always go smoothly. There was one time when one of my writers who was very high-strung came up with a joke that I didn't think was funny. He jumped up and started to argue with me. He said, "I know it's funny! I told it at a party last night and had the people screaming!"

I said, "After three martinis it might be funny, but in this room it isn't."

Well, the veins in the guy's neck popped out, his face turned red, and he started pounding my desk, hollering, "George, I've been a comedy writer all my life, and I know this is a very funny joke, and it's going to get a tremendous laugh!"

By now he was screaming right in my face. I smiled sweetly and said, "You're cute when you get mad."

He stormed out of the office, and that took care of the writing for that day. The next morning when he came in, before he had a chance to say anything I said, "You're right. I thought the joke over; it's a funny joke and I'm going to use it."

He jumped up again and his face turned red. "Don't! I told that joke last night in a bar and it didn't get a snicker! It only proves that you know nothing about humor!"

I told you things don't always go smoothly.

The next writer I'm going to tell you about is not easy to describe. But before I try, let me say this about him; his name is Norman Paul and he's one hell of a writer. There's not a comedy series on the air that wouldn't like to hire him. He's not only a good joke writer, but he has a marvelous story mind and is a fine constructionist. You know, sometimes when you're writing a script you'll be right in the middle of it and find yourself up a blind alley with nowhere to go. Well, whenever we found ourselves in that kind of a spot we'd struggle with it for a while, and finally I'd say, "Fellows, let's break it up. We'll try again in the morning."

I never gave it another thought and had a good night's sleep, because I knew that in the morning Norman would have the solution—and he never disappointed me. His mind was always on the script, whether he was sitting in a bar, driving his car, sitting in a bar, relaxing at home, sitting in a bar, eating at a pizzeria, or maybe even sitting in a bar— he never stopped thinking.

Now that I've said all these nice things about Norman, let me try to describe him. He's really a very good looking man, but he does his best to disguise it. If Norman stood up, he'd be about six feet tall, but he always walks around in sort of a half crouch. He looks like he's taking a bow and nobody's applauding.

About Norman's clothes. He never wears a necktie, and his suit looks like he just sent it out to have it wrinkled. He wears his pants a little below his stomach, so they hang down and appear to be about five inches too long for him. This is good because they cover up his socks, which never match. His shoes are so scuffed up they look like he had somebody break them in for him at a lumber camp. I don't know where Norman buys his clothes, but the guy who sells them to him must have a hell of a sense of humor.

One thing Norman is proud of is his full head of wavy hair. It's beautiful. However, when you look at the overall picture his hair looks like it should be on somebody else's head. Now, in describing Norman Paul I admit that I did exaggerate a little bit. In all fairness I'd like to say that he came in one day and his socks did match.

Norman always drives a car that looks exactly like he does. The reason is that Norman's mind is so absorbed in his work he can't be bothered with trifles. When he buys a car he never has it serviced. He puts in gasoline, but he never checks the tires, changes the oil, or puts in water. He just drives it until it stops running and then he buys a new one. The back seat of his car always looks like a mobile disaster area. It's cluttered with old scripts, newspapers, magazines, discarded clothing, a half-eaten ham sandwich, anything Norman happens to throw back there.

One day he was driving down Santa Monica Boulevard and he flicked a cigarette out the window, but it blew into the back seat. Well, naturally all that debris back there caught on fire, but Norman didn't even notice it. Other drivers were honking and hollering and waving at him, but he drove for three blocks before he finally noticed his car was on fire. He was concentrating on how to finish a story line, so a fire meant nothing to him. He drove into a gas station, they put out the fire, he left the car there, and bought a new one.

When Norman worked for me I always made sure I had a full-length couch in the office. That's the only way he could write; lying on his back and looking up at the ceiling. One day I said to him, "Norman, why don't you stand up for a while, you're pressing all the wrinkles out of your suit." He never even heard me; he was figuring out how to start the next scene.

Norman was a very sensitive man, who didn't accept criticism too well. He was always quitting his job. I'd say he quit me about three times a week, sometimes three times a day. I was always able to calm him down and we'd go back to work, but on one day things got more heated than usual. I don't know what we were arguing about, but we finished up screaming at each other. Finally Norman jumped up off the couch, shouting, "I know I've quit before, but this time I mean it!" And out he walked. Well, I walked out with him. When we got to the parking lot Norman turned to me and said, "What are you doing here?"

I said, "Well, as long as you quit, I figured I'd quit, too."

Five minutes later Norman was back on the couch and we were working again.

I must have upset Norman a lot, because no matter how hard he tried he just couldn't quit me. One day after work Norman stopped off at a bar to have a drink, and while the bartender was making it Norman's foot accidentally slipped off the bar rail and he broke his ankle. That's the story that Norman told us; the bartender probably had a different version.

Anyway, the next morning Norman's wife, Kay, pushed him into the office in a wheelchair. His leg was in a cast up to his knee. We all helped get him on the couch, and then Kay left, saying she'd pick him up later in the day. Well, after we ran out of broken-leg jokes we all settled down and went to work. Within twenty minutes Norman and I were at it again; another one of our silly arguments that ended up with Norman hollering, "I can't take this anymore! I quit!"

You should have seen him try to quit. He'd forgotten he had the cast on his leg and he couldn't get off the couch. He floundered around like a beached whale. We just sat there looking at him. Finally I said, "Okay, Norman, you're not working for me anymore, so would you please lie there and be quiet. The other fellows and I have a script to get out." So we ignored him and went to work. Well, Norman couldn't stand it. In no time he was in there pitching jokes with the rest of us.

"Norman," I said, "don't you want to save those funny lines for your next job? You're not on salary anymore."

He grumbled, "Well, I can't just lie here like a dummy. When Kay comes to get me then I'll quit."

We finished out the day with no more problems. When Kay came we all helped Norman into the chair, and while she was wheeling him out I said, "Norman, you want me to write a little farewell note on your cast?"

For the first time that day Norman laughed. He said, "George, I'll see you in the morning."

Well, Norman was in that cast for six weeks, and during that time he didn't quit me once because he couldn't. The first day he walked into the office without the cast I said to him, "Norman, these past six weeks have been the most pleasant we've ever spent together. If you were any kind of a sport, you'd go back to that same bar and break your other leg."

Norman and I went on like that for years. The more we fought, the more we liked each other. He never really did quit me. When I stopped producing television shows Norman went on to other things. However, he still drops by the office every once in a while, and I'm always glad to see him. I know we haven't stopped liking each other because we still argue. And I'm sure when Norman finishes reading about himself in this book he'll throw it into the back seat of his car.

In terms of time there was one writer who was with me longer than any of the others. His name was Harvey Helm. I'd say he wrote for me about thirty-five years. He started by selling me loose jokes in vaudeville and stayed with me through radio and television right up until Gracie retired. Harvey was more than a writer, he was a personal friend. He and his wife, Ruth, and Gracie and myself used to go out socially all the time.

One time the four of us spent a week's vacation in Honolulu. Gracie and I were very big in radio then, and our sponsor was Chesterfield cigarettes. When we arrived in Honolulu naturally the press interviewed us. One of the reporters asked me what was my first impression of Honolulu. I had an answer right on the tip of my tongue. I said, "Seeing Diamond Head was very exciting. I've never seen a volcano before, but if it smokes again, I hope it smokes Chesterfields."

That line was picked up by the wire services and printed in papers all over the country. It made my sponsor very happy, and everybody thought I was a great wit for ad-libbing a line like that. What I didn't tell them was that Harvey Helm gave it to me the night before.

The same thing happened in New York City when Billy Rose opened his big hit musical, *Jumbo*. For one reason or another the opening had been delayed for almost a year. When I arrived at the theater I was interviewed for radio. I said, "I'm looking forward to seeing *Jumbo*, and I only hope it stays open as long as it stayed closed."

I had scored again. I got so I could ad-lib without looking at the paper that Harvey wrote it on.

When it came to writing, Harvey had a wild, wild imagination. His jokes were perfect for Gracie's character, and the words he put in her mouth made sense, but only to Gracie. I doubt if any writer ever worked the way Harvey did. He'd sit for hours at a typewriter, a cigarette dangling from his lips, and thumb through a copy of *Popular Mechanics* magazine. The magazine was full of pictures, and that's where Harvey got his inspirations for those mad jokes he'd write. Let me give you a few samples of what Harvey came up with. Now, you may have heard some of these jokes, but when Harvey wrote them they were new:

A picture of a plastic swimming pool inspired this one:

GRACIE: My sister Hazel just put a new swimming pool in her backyard. Yesterday we had a marvelous time swimming and diving. And tomorrow we'll even have more fun when they put water in it.

When he saw a picture of a glassblower he came up with this:

GRACIE: My brother Willy got into trouble on account of his new job. He's a glassblower, and yesterday he got the hiccups and blew himself into a bottle.

Then he saw a picture of a saxophone:

GRACIE: My brother's taking a correspondence course on how to play the saxophone and he's going to be very good at it. Every night he blows his lesson into an envelope and mails it to the teacher.

179

This one came from an ad for an iron grill door:

GRACIE: My uncle Harry just got out of jail because he's a great artist. He painted a picture of an open window on the wall of his cell, and when the guard came in to close the window, uncle Harry walked out the door.

Antique salt and pepper shakers:

GRACIE: The reason I put the salt in the pepper shaker, and the pepper in the salt shaker is that people are always getting them mixed up. Now when they get mixed up they'll be right.

Well, that was Harvey Helm's mind at work!

But Harvey didn't get all of his inspirations out of *Popular Mechanics*. A lot of it came out of a bottle. I can honestly say that Harvey used to drink a little. Well, as long as I'm going to be honest, Harvey didn't drink a little—he drank a lot. Most of the time he held his liquor very well. When he first came to work for me I didn't know whether he was drinking or not. There's an old line that describes Harvey in those days: "I never knew he drank until one day he showed up sober."

Having Harvey work for you was a very nerve-racking experience. But in the long run it was worth it. He'd go along okay for a while, and then he'd go off the deep end and disappear for a couple of weeks, and then into a sanatorium to dry out. He'd be fine for a few months, then the same thing would happen again. One time in New York after one of his escapades, Harvey showed up at my hotel room in bad shape. I called Dr. Leo Schoenfeld, who was not only a well-known society doctor, but a close personal friend of mine. I asked him if he would come over and pick up Harvey and check him into Bellevue Hospital in order to get him sobered up. Dr. Schoenfeld didn't want any part of it, but as a favor to me he finally agreed. He called the hospital and arranged for Harvey to be admitted. A half hour later he had Harvey in a taxi and they were on their way to Bellevue.

Well, Harvey wasn't ready to spend four days in Bellevue,

so he pulled himself together just long enough to put that tricky little mind of his to work. While Dr. Schoenfeld was paying off the cabdriver, Harvey rushed into the hospital and up to the admission desk. Assuming a very dignified manner, he said to the nurse in charge, "I'm Dr. Leo Schoenfeld."

The nurse said, "Oh, yes, Doctor, I got your call. Where's your patient, Harvey Helm?"

Just at that moment Dr. Schoenfeld was coming through the door, so Harvey pointed to him, saying, "That's him. I suggest you rush him right upstairs before he becomes violent."

Before Dr. Schoenfeld knew what hit him, two burly interns grabbed him and hustled him into an elevator, and he was gone. In the meantime Harvey got into a cab, and I didn't hear from him for two weeks. However, I did hear from Dr. Schoenfeld. He sent me a bill, and it was a very sizable one. But it was two years before I could get Leo to speak to me again.

A strange thing about Harvey was that he was always terribly concerned about any friend who had a drinking problem. One morning he came to work very upset. He said, "George, I had a horrible experience last night. You remember Joe Talbot?"

I said, "Sure, an actor. He worked for me a few times."

Worriedly, Harvey said, "Well, I ran into him in a bar last night, and he was so loaded he didn't know where he was. I had to carry him home, undress him, put him to bed, and call the doctor."

I had always liked Joe Talbot, so I asked, "I'm sorry to hear that, how was he when you left him?"

Harvey shook his head and said, "Not good, George. When the doctor got there he asked him if he saw anything like pink elephants, or blue mice, or purple alligators, but Joe said no. That's why I'm so worried, George. The room was full of them!" I knew right then that Harvey was getting ready for another trip.

181

This may all sound funny now, but it wasn't funny when it happened. But, in spite of all the troubles, I often wish I could have gotten my other writers to do a little drinking, because Harvey's stuff was the greatest.

My younger brother, Willy Burns, belongs in this chapter because he worked with all the writers I had over the years. Willy wasn't the kind of a writer who put a piece of paper in a typewriter and knocked out a scene, but he was great in a room where everybody would sit around and pitch funny lines. But besides contributing to the scripts, Willy also handled all my business activities. He checked all my contracts to see that they were drawn up right, he okayed all my bookings, he set up interviews with the press, and when I played Las Vegas he would go up there and make sure everything was right. To sum it up, Willy ran interference for me so I didn't have to worry about anything except writing and performing.

Willy did so many things for me that it often conflicted with his writing. There was one time when we were writing a scene that took place in a hospital. It was all about our neighbor, Harry Morton, going in for an operation. Well, in the middle of it Willy got a phone call and had to go see my lawyer in Beverly Hills. While he was gone we decided the scene in the hospital wouldn't work so we threw it out. Two hours later, when Willy got back, he was all excited. He said, "George, I've got a great finish for that scene in the hospital."

I said, "Well, I hope it works in a car wash."

Willy shrugged his shoulders and said, "I get it. You switched the scene. Instead of a hospital it's now a car wash. Well, that takes care of that great finish I thought of."

I said, "Don't feel bad, Willy, we'll try to get Harry Morton in a hospital before the season is over."

Poor Willy had another function that I'm sure he didn't enjoy. Whenever I would get mad at one of the writers I'd scream at Willy. I didn't dare scream at the writer, because

182

he was liable to quit me, but I knew Willy understood me. When my temper flares up I holler and shout, but in a minute it's over. And when I'm hollering I have no idea what I'm talking about.

One day when things were going slow and we weren't getting anywhere I went into my hollering bit. I jumped up and started shouting at Willy, and I got so confused I ended up by yelling, "Damn it, Willy, just don't sit there wearing those same red socks again, come up with something!"

He leaned back in his chair, and with a little smile, said, "George, the only one in the room wearing red socks is Packy."

I sputtered and stammered, and finally said, "Well, put on Packy's red socks and come up with something!" Everybody laughed, and by then I was all sputtered out. In a calm voice I said, "I guess that was pretty funny. Now let's see if we can think of something that funny to put in the script."

Willy's favorite recreation was gambling. He loved to go to Las Vegas. He'd shoot craps, play blackjack, roulette, baccarat, and he had a real knack for it—he knew how to lose at every game. But I guess his greatest love was playing the horses, and he considered himself an expert at handicapping. With this he had a soulmate in the man on the couch, Norman Paul. When we were working and I had to leave the room to go to the bathroom, out would come the Racing Form and they'd call their bets into the bookmaker. I knew what was going on, so every morning at exactly ten thirty I went to the bathroom, ready or not. Sometimes I'd just stand there and wash my hands for ten minutes. I was afraid if they didn't get all their bets down, they wouldn't be able to concentrate on writing the next scene. When I came back from the bathroom I'd always hum a few bars so they'd know I was coming and have time to hang up the phone and put the Racing Form away.

When four guys are sitting in a room trying to write comedy, the toughest part is to get started. Once you get a hook on the scene everybody begins to talk at once, and the jokes come so fast there isn't time to write them down. Well, one morning we were sitting there and nothing happened. There was complete silence; we just couldn't seem to get rolling. After about an hour of looking at one another, I said, "Fellows, we've got a script to finish. Now if somebody doesn't get funny pretty soon, I'm not going to the bathroom at ten thirty." That did the trick. At ten thirty I was back in the bathroom as usual washing my hands again.

Willy was with me practically from the time I started doing well in show business. I must tell you one cute story that happened when I was working with Gracie, but before we were married. At that time I was already in love with Gracie, but she was in love with Benny Ryan. Well, we were playing in Cleveland, and Gracie had a small two-room suite in the hotel and I was living with Willy. One night after the show Gracie insisted she was going to cook dinner for us. Now, a cook Gracie wasn't, but she decided to fix a big platter of spaghetti and tomato sauce. I happen to know that when you make tomato sauce you put in two or three of those little white peppers, and you put them in whole to give the sauce a tang. Gracie didn't know that. She put in about ten peppers and sliced them open, which released all that heat.

She had made an occasion of it because this was the first time she'd ever cooked dinner for us. There were two little candles burning on the table, flowers, a bottle of red wine, soft music—she'd gone all out. Well, Willy and I had a couple of drinks, and finally Gracie announced that dinner was ready. We sat down at the table, and in she came with this big platter of spaghetti covered with tomato sauce. Can I tell you something? The sauce on that spaghetti was so strong that it could have come in by itself.

Gracie served both of us a heaping plateful and then went back to the kitchen for the salad. Willy and I both took a mouthful and then turned and looked at each other. Willy's ears had turned a bright red, and I could feel the fillings

184

melting out of my teeth. After Willy finally got his breath back, he gasped, "George, this sauce is so hot I can't eat it! I'm going to go! You make some excuse to Gracie."

I said, "Willy, you can't walk out."

Barely able to whisper, Willy said, "Oh, yes I can. You're the one who can't walk out. If you don't eat that spaghetti, she'll marry Benny Ryan."

I whispered back, "And if you don't eat that spaghetti, you'll be looking for another job."

At that point in came Gracie with the salad and sat down at the table. Willy and I started on our salads, carefully avoiding the spaghetti. Gracie took a big mouthful of spaghetti, and both Willy and I stopped and stared at her, waiting for her reaction. It wasn't long in coming. She sat there unable to speak. Finally, smiling bravely through the tears streaming down her cheeks, she managed to say, "This tastes terrible—I didn't put enough peppers in the sauce. Let's go to a Chinese restaurant and have dinner."

Willy picked up his glass of wine and said, "I'll drink to that," and off we went.

That happened a long time ago. Willy passed away in 1966, and I miss him very much. And just in case you're interested, before that television season was over we did do the scene where Harry Morton went into the hospital for an operation—and we used Willy's finish.

Memoirs of a Warmed-Over Casanova

It's amazing to me how many people seem to be interested in my love life. I've been giving a lot of interviews lately, and the first question they ask is usually, "Is it true that you only go out with young girls?" Well, I'd like to clear that point up once and for all—it is not true. Sometimes I go out with a girl who's twenty or twenty-one. But I guess Warren Beatty, Robert Redford, Jack Nicholson, Paul Newman, and Burt Reynolds all get asked the same question. It's just something us sex symbols have to learn to live with.

I promised the publisher of this book that I'd hold nothing back, so I'm going to let my hair down. I not only can let my hair down, I can walk away and leave it there. But to me a promise is a promise, so here are the facts. In my long and checkered career I've loved many women. There was Clara Bow, Nita Naldi, Vilma Banky, Dorothy Gish and her kid sister Lillian, Pola Negri, Valeska Surratt, Helen Hayes, and Garbo. I loved them all! I never met them, but I loved them! So at last it's out in the open. Now I hope the press will stop hounding me.

But in all seriousness, the only real love in my life was Gracie, and I was happily married to her for thirty-eight years. After she was gone it took a long time before I even thought about going out with anybody else. And when I did start dating it was never with a thought of serious involvement. I had a wonderful marriage, and I don't intend to get married again.

187

Going out with a girl now and then is enjoyable—someone to have dinner with, to take to the theater, to watch television with, someone to talk to and— Now, there's a reason why I prefer going out with young girls to older women. If I decide to spend an evening at home watching television with a girl my age (and there are very few girls my age left), I don't think it's very interesting for her. I love to watch old movies, and chances are she's already seen it before, so she'd be bored. On the other hand, with a young girl all the old movies are brand new, so if I happen to doze off, she can still enjoy herself.

Before any of you readers get the wrong idea about me, I'd better clear something up. I do not chase after girls, and I do not try to pick up any girls. You'll never find me cruising down Sunset Boulevard with the top down; I do not hang out in bars offering to buy drinks; and I certainly don't put ads in the *Free Press* enumerating my charms. I'm just like the grandfather of the boy next door.

What I'm trying to say is the girls I go out with are girls I've met through friends, or girls I've worked with. For instance, some time ago I did a television show in New York. It was a musical show, and one of the dancers in the show was a charming little girl named Debbie Phillips. Well, during the four days of rehearsal we got to know each other, and before I left I told her if she happened to get to California to be sure and give me a call. I didn't think any more about it until a month later my phone rang and there she was. I asked her if she'd like to go out to dinner that night and she said yes. You see, you don't have to cruise down Sunset Boulevard with your top down to get a date.

Anyway, Debbie and I went out that night and we had a marvelous time. For the next six months we saw a lot of each other. She was very attractive, she had a good sense of humor, and she always woke me up when the movie was over.

Then one day I got a phone call from her and she was all excited. She told me she was going back East to get married

188

to the fellow she used to go with. She thanked me for all the good times we'd had together, I wished her the best of luck with her marriage, and that was the end of it. Of course, I did miss Debbie, I missed her very much. It's no fun sleeping through an old movie and having nobody to wake you up. Then I finally bought an alarm clock and I didn't miss her anymore.

Now, that should be the end of that story, right? Well, you don't know my sincere but misguided friend, George Pallay. You may remember him earlier in the book—he's the fellow who told everybody the young girls he went out with were his nieces. Well, Pallay is a perennial romanticist. I'd say that he falls madly in love at least once a month, and twice on Fridays. And every time one of these romances is over he goes to pieces. He can't eat, he can't sleep, his whole world comes to an end. He can't find a building tall enough to jump off. When he goes through one of these experiences he refers to it as "carrying a torch," which I think is a very quaint phrase for a seventy-five-year-old man.

Anyway, the same week that Debbie left I was booked to do a television show in Toronto. At that time Pallay was in Miami, but somehow he got the news that Debbie and I had split up. He assumed that my splitup would affect me the same way that his always affected him, so he caught the first plane to Toronto to save me from killing myself.

Meanwhile, during my television rehearsals I met a bouncy little French-Canadian girl, Yvonne, who was the assistant to the producer, and we were having lunch up in my suite. We finished lunch and she went into the bathroom to freshen up, and right about then Pallay came bursting into the room. He rushed over to me, put his arm around my shoulder, and said, "George, I just got the news about your breakup with Debbie. I know how you feel so I'm going to stay right here with you all week."

We hadn't even said hello yet, but he kept rambling on. "I've been through all this myself, and there's only one way

189

you're going to get over it. You've got to forget Debbie and look around for somebody else! And believe me, George, you'll meet another girl in no time!"

Just then Yvonne walked out of the bathroom. I said, "Pallay, is that fast enough?"

Pallay just stood there staring at Yvonne with his mouth open. I introduced him to her, and she went back to work. After she left, Pallay said, "I really admire you, George, pretending that you're interested in that little French girl. It takes a lot of courage to put up such a great front when I know you feel terrible on the inside!"

"You're right, Pallay," I said. "I shouldn't have had that cucumber salad for lunch."

A smile came across his face. He shook his head and said, "George, I don't know how you do it. Standing there with a broken heart and you can still make jokes."

Even though he was sincere, I was starting to get a little sick to my stomach. I said, "Look, Pallay, I've got to do a television show in an hour. Now, if everything goes well and the audience likes me, you and Yvonne and I will all go out to dinner. But if it's a bad audience and I don't get any laughs, I want you to find the tallest building in Toronto and you and I will go up to the top, we'll hold hands, and we'll jump off together."

Well, it turned out to be a good audience, and Pallay, Yvonne, and I had dinner that night. And during the week Yvonne introduced him to her sister. It's the first time Pallay ever had a French niece.

Being an eligible bachelor in Beverly Hills made me very much in demand. Whenever there was a party and one of my friends had to be out of town, it wasn't unusual for him to call me and ask if I'd mind taking his wife. Well, this was fine with me because I like parties. I'd not only take his wife, but I'd take my music with me in case there was a piano player there. Whenever I took Danny Kaye's wife,

Sylvia, to a party, I didn't have to bring my music because she knew how to play in my key.

One time the Irving Lazars took over the upstairs room at the Bistro for a private dinner dance. The day of the party Mary Lazar called me and asked if I would pick up Cyd Charisse because Tony Martin was playing Las Vegas. It turned out to be a wonderful evening because Cyd is great to dance with. Once when we were out on the floor dancing, the band went into "La Vie en Rose." Well, that's one of my big numbers, so I sang it into Cyd's ear. When I finished the first chorus, I whispered, "Cyd, you've made movies with Fred Astaire, who's a great dancer, and you're married to Tony Martin, who's a great singer—it must be very exciting for you to be on a dance floor with a combination of both." She started laughing so hard we couldn't even finish the dance! I must be a great comedian—I get laughs even when I'm serious.

One of the first times I took a friend's wife to a party was when Jean Negulesco's wife, Dusty, called me and asked me to be her escort. Jean was in Spain at that time directing a picture, so I told Dusty I'd be glad to. This was before I had much practice taking out married women, so at the end of the evening the "eligible bachelor" almost made an idiot of himself.

Anyway, we had a lot of fun at the party, and at one o'clock I drove Dusty home. I pulled my car into her driveway, and she said, "George, would you like to come in for a martini?"

I said, "Dusty, it's one o'clock in the morning!"

She looked at me with sort of a puzzled expression. "Is there some Beverly Hills law that says you can't drink a martini at one o'clock in the morning?"

"No," I answered, "but at this hour a martini seems so—so intimate."

Dusty laughed and said, "Oh, George, stop acting like Andy Hardy. I know it's wicked, but nobody will ever know that you and I had a martini at one o'clock in the morning. My help is off—my husband's in Spain—and I'm sure my cocker spaniel will keep his mouth shut." So I went in, we had a martini, I said goodnight, and went home. But the next day it was all over Beverly Hills. Do you know that cocker spaniel blew the whistle on us!

Rosalind Russell is one of the first ladies of film. She has a great sense of humor, she's very witty and always a delight to be with. I'm glad her husband, Freddie Brisson, is out of town so much because I really enjoy taking Roz out. One morning after taking her to one of these parties, Freddie called me on the phone. "George," he said, "I just flew in from New York, and I want to thank you for taking Roz out last night. She's still talking about what a terrific dancer you are."

"It's easy to be a terrific dancer, Freddie," I said, "all you have to do is hold the girl very close with your right hand and she's got to follow you."

He said, "George, who are you kidding? I've seen you dance, and the reason you hold them close is you're a very sexy dancer."

"Freddie," I said, "I don't want you to tell this to Roz, but being sexy had nothing to do with it. The reason I hold them close is at my age I've got to hang on to something!"

That's what I told Freddie Brisson, but when he reads this he'll find out he was absolutely right—I *am* a very sexy dancer.

There was one dinner party I went to alone, and at dinner I found myself seated between Pamela Mason and Zsa Zsa Gabor. Everybody was telling jokes and anecdotes, and it was a very gay table. I didn't know Zsa Zsa too well then, so I directed most of my stories to her because she got to laughing so hard she started to hiccup. Well, after three or four minutes she still couldn't get rid of them.

"Vy don't von of you dahlings frighten me so I can get rid of my hiccups," she gasped in between them.

192

Well, I wanted to be helpful, so I took her hand and put it under the table on the napkin in my lap. She pulled her hand away and jumped up indignantly. "Mr. Burns, you're a very naughty man!" Then she thought a moment and smiled down at me. "But I forgive you, dahling, you cured my hiccups!"

That surprised me. I never thought a napkin would shock Zsa Zsa.

Relating these party incidents reminds me of something that happened while I was still married to Gracie. She had gone up to San Francisco to visit her sister Hazel, so I went by myself to a party we were invited to in Sherman Oaks. Sophie Tucker was there, and she was alone, too, so at the end of the evening she asked me to drive her home. Well, I'd known Sophie practically all my life, so on the way home I thought I'd be funny and get a little laugh. Driving along Mulholland Drive, I pulled the car over to a secluded spot and turned off the engine. "Sophie," I said, "we're out of gas—let's neck."

She just looked at me, and without cracking a smile, she said, "George, we're both out of gas, let's go."

I said, "Sophie, you're not laughing, didn't you think that was funny?"

"Of course," she answered, "what I said was very funny, and thanks for the straight line."

Well, we both laughed and I drove her home. But I never pulled that gag again. I hate to be topped twice in the same evening.

Now, aside from acting as an escort for his friends' wives, the eligible bachelor has to think of himself once in a while. For the last two years I've been sharing myself with two charming young ladies, Lita Baron and Joanna Baer. They're both very pretty, and they fit in beautifully no matter where you take them.

I met Lita Baron at a party given by Mr. and Mrs. Harry Jameson. The Jamesons are famous for their lavish formal parties, and they always serve squab for dinner. That evening I happened to be sitting next to Lita, but we hadn't been introduced, so I thought I'd break the ice. I looked over at her and said, "Miss Baron, I couldn't help admiring your squab."

She gave me a look, then she laughed and said, "Yours is cute, too."

Now I doubt if that's the way the Duke of Windsor introduced himself to Wally Simpson, but it worked for me, and Lita and I have been sharing our squab ever since. I always enjoy going out with Lita because she enjoys me. Everything I say makes her laugh, and it's good for my ego. When I'm around her I think I'm one of the great comedians. And when I use those same lines on somebody else I think I'm back in Altoona again.

Lita is a very social person; she knows everybody in Hollywood and remembers all their names. This is great for me because I can't remember my own name. Whenever we'd be sitting in a restaurant and somebody we knew would start over to our table, she'd whisper their name in my ear so I wouldn't be embarrassed. Her always leaning close to me like that gave people the idea that we were very lovey-dovey. One time it even landed us on the front page of a newspaper. There was a picture of us having dinner at Chasen's, and the caption underneath said, "It must be serious between Lita Baron and George Burns. As usual Lita is whispering sweet nothings into George's ear!" Actually she wasn't whispering sweet nothings at all. She was saying, "George, that man coming towards you is your brother Willy."

When I first started dating Lita I was amazed at the size of her wardrobe. Every time we went out she wore a different gown. I don't ever remember her wearing the same dress twice, and they were all beautiful. She always looked so dressed up that I felt I had to get dressed up, too. Well, if there's anything I hate it's getting dressed up. I like to look as good as I can, but I'm much more comfortable when I'm dressed casual. In fact, I prefer going to restaurants where I don't even have to wear a tie. Can you imagine us walking into a place with Lita in one of those gorgeous outfits and me in an open sport shirt? People would think she was taking her gardener out to dinner.

This went on for months. Every time we went out I wore a dark suit and tie, and it makes me nervous to wear a dark suit and a dark tie. I always get the feeling there are eight guys in back of me waiting for me to lie down.

Anyway, one night we were going out to dinner, so I went over to her house to pick her up. Naturally I was wearing my Utter-McKinley outfit. But when Lita opened the door I got a real surprise. There she stood, wearing blue jeans, a pullover sweater, loafers, and her hair tied back with a little ribbon. She looked absolutely darling, but I'd never seen her that way before. I said, "Lita, did you forget we were going out to dinner tonight?"

Hesitantly she said, "George . . . I don't know how to tell you this . . . but I'm getting tired of getting all dressed up every time you take me out. I know how you always love to get dressed up, but just once couldn't we be casual?"

I couldn't believe my ears. "Lita," I said, "as long as you feel that way, from now on we'll always dress casual. And I'm going to do something I've never done for any other girl—even though it's my favorite, I'll never wear this black suit again."

She put her arms around me and gave me a kiss. "George," she said, "you're so considerate." I was kind of sorry she didn't have the hiccups.

Anyway, we stopped by my house, I got into some comfortable clothes, and we went to a quiet little restaurant called Dominick's and had a wonderful evening.

Now let me tell you about the girl who shared the other half of me during that time. I met Joanna Baer over the telephone. She was working for Michael Viner, the man who produced my concert at the Shubert Theater in Los Angeles, and for weeks I knew her only as a voice. Well, I'm not stupid, I figured there must be a body to go with that voice, so I invited her to lunch. And I was right, there was a body—and what a body—tall, dark-haired, beautiful, voluptuous, and she had a driver's license. That's important. I won't go out with a girl unless she can drive me.

Now, Lita and Joanna had something in common; Lita was married to Rory Calhoun, and Joanna was married to Max Baer, Jr., and both husbands were very tall, handsome, virile men. It was only natural that after their divorces the girls went for me; I'm not tall, I'm not handsome, and I'm certainly not virile, but who wants to take out a girl who has no imagination?

I never met a girl who was interested in as many things as Joanna. She flies an airplane, she designs her own clothes, she's a great cook, she's a plumber, an electrician, a carpenter, and she built the house she's living in. She's the only girl I know who ever came to my house with a tool kit.

But there was never anything for Joanna to fix when she came over. Daniel, the man who works for me, can do everything, so everything in my house is always in perfect order. Well, this upset Joanna, because she wanted to fix my toilet to prove that she loved me. To show you what a nice man I am, the next time my plumbing broke down I told Daniel not to touch it. That night when Joanna came over I let her work on it. She was so happy to fix my toilet that she thought we were engaged. Well, I admit that's a slight exaggeration, but now that I'm an author I sometimes take a few literary liberties. But Joanna's still the prettiest plumber I've ever seen.

It was always a joy to go out with Joanna because I never had to move a muscle. Whenever we'd go out in the evening she'd always drive the car. I recall one evening we were going to a party at Jim and Henny Backus' house in Bel Air. About halfway up the hill all of a sudden the car sputtered and stopped. Well, I just sat there; I know nothing about cars. Sometimes even when I blow the horn I get my finger caught in the crack. I turned to Joanna and said, "What's wrong?"

"I think your regulator's off," she answered.

Well, I couldn't pass that up! I said, "My regulator's been off for years, but why did the car stop?" She never even heard that comical line; she was already out of the car with her head under the hood.

Right about then a car pulled up, and two good-looking young fellows got out. Now, get this picture: There I was sitting in a dinner jacket, smoking a cigar, and a beautiful girl in a white, clinging evening gown was under the hood. In a cocky voice one of the fellows said, "Look, doll, when you're through fixing your grandfather's car, how'd you like to go out with us?"

Joanna raised her head and, looking right at this kid, she said, "I'm nobody's doll, and that's not my grandfather, that's my date. Now if you two clowns don't split, you're both asking for a karate chop!"

I forgot to mention, she does that, too. But while all this was going on I was a nervous wreck. I rolled up the window and caught my finger in it. And it hurt, because it was the same one I usually catch in the horn.

Now, don't get the idea from my pathetic literary liberties that Joanna is anything but a beautiful, feminine girl. And what's more, she looks absolutely marvelous on a dance floor. I enjoy dancing with her because again I do absolutely nothing. I stand there and sway to the music, then I push Joanna out, and she spins and twirls and circles the whole dance floor and eventually comes back to me. Sometimes I push her out and sit down, and when she finishes circling and comes back I get up and give her another push. I don't like to brag, but when it comes to pushing I'm in a class with Gene Kelly.

One of my more memorable evenings with Joanna started with dinner at The Luau, which is a very popular Polynesian restaurant in Beverly Hills. We started drinking an

Aku-Aku, which is a rum drink served in a hollowed-out coconut shell, and you sip it through a straw. It's full of shaved ice and tastes like a fruit punch, but it's very potent. I don't know why, but I was feeling good and having fun, so I drank three. In the middle of my third Aku-Aku without my knowing it my necktie had fallen into the coconut and froze there. So when I got up to go to the men's room, the coconut went with me.

Well, it turned into one of those silly evenings in which everything seems funny. After dinner Joanna drove me to my house, where she usually picked up her car and drove on home. But this time when we got to the front door and I took out my house key, it slipped out of my hand and fell into the grass. It was very dark, so the two of us got down on our hands and knees and started groping around the grass trying to find the key. What with the rum and this ridiculous situation, Joanna and I got to giggling. All of a sudden the beam of a flashlight hit us, and when we looked up there stood a Beverly Hills policeman. He looked at us for a moment, then shaking his head he said, "Mr. Burns, I've heard of people smoking grass, but I never saw anybody eating it before." That's what I like about living in Beverly Hills, we have very funny policemen.

I still see Joanna, and I still see Lita Baron. When I go out with Lita I dress casual, and when I take out Joanna I stay away from rum and I make sure my house key is on a chain.

And There Was Lisa

During the last several years I've taken out a lot of girls. I've enjoyed being with every one of them, and they always told me they enjoyed being with me. They had to—I told them I was very sensitive, and they didn't want to see an old man cry. But long before I started dating all these girls there was one girl in particular who played a very important role in my life for about three years. Her name was Lisa Miller, and I met her when she was eighteen years old. Now, don't ask me how Lisa and I got together in the first place, because I really don't know. It just seemed to happen.

I was playing an engagement at the Riviera Hotel in Las Vegas, and on the bill was a group called "The Kids Next Door." It was a group of seventeen young singers, and Lisa was one of them. They opened the show and then I'd follow them. I always came down a little early because they all wanted to make it big in show business and I enjoyed watching them work. To me they were a bunch of nice-looking kids who all looked alike until one night after the early show. I was on my way to change clothes when I heard somebody playing the piano in my dressing room. I couldn't imagine who it was, and besides they were playing "The Maple Leaf Rag," which goes back to the turn of the century. I thought maybe one of my old buddies like Teddy Roosevelt had come backstage to surprise me. I opened the door and walked in, and there was Lisa.

When she heard me come in she stopped playing and looked up a little apprehensively. "I'm sorry, Mr. Burns," she said, "I hope you don't mind my using your piano while you were onstage."

"No, I don't mind," I said, "but what I'd like to know is how a young girl like you would know the 'Maple Leaf Rag.'"

With a smile Lisa said, "My mother taught it to me, and my grandmother taught it to my mother."

I thought I'd have a little fun with the kid, so I said, "Well, maybe you could get your grandmother to teach it to me."

She came back with, "I'll try, but it will have to be in the afternoon when my grandfather isn't home. He's a very jealous man." And out she went.

I was sort of amused, but I didn't think any more of it. Then the next afternoon I decided to kill some time before the first show, so I went down to the casino to play a little blackjack. I played along for a while, then I remember I had a hand with a ten in the hole and a four showing, so I asked for another card. The dealer hit me with a nine, and I busted out. Just then I heard a voice behind me say, "Mr. Burns, when you've got fourteen and the dealer has a five showing, you should never ask for another card."

I looked over my shoulder and there stood Maple Leaf Rag. And she was right, so I said, "Look, kid, how do you know so much about blackjack?"

With a straight face she said, "My mother taught me, and my grandmother—"

Well, I wasn't going through the grandfather bit again, so I stopped her. "Hold it, kid. If you know so much about blackjack, I've got thirty dollars left. Sit down and play for me." And she did. I stood there and watched her, and this kid played blackjack better than she did "Maple Leaf Rag." Within fifteen minutes she'd won $200. I said, "You really know what you're doing, kid."

She smiled at me and said, "Mr. Burns, my name isn't kid, it's Lisa Miller."

I said, "Well, the way you play blackjack your name

200

should be Nick the Greek." I picked up the chips and offered her some. "You won two hundred dollars, so half of these are yours."

"No, no," she said, "Thanks, but it was your money and I wouldn't think of it."

Well, I thought the least I could do was invite her to dinner, so I asked her to join Charlie Reade, my road manager, and me for a late supper that night. After the show Charlie and I sat at a table in the dining room, and I began to wonder if Lisa would show up or not. Well, I'd no sooner taken a sip of my martini when I looked up and there was Lisa, coming into the room. And when Lisa comes into a room, you know she's there. She's very animated and vivacious, and there's something very alive about her. As she crossed to the table I got my first really good look at her. Lisa's a tall girl, about 5'8", with straight blond hair, large blue eyes, and a mischievous smile.

She sat down with Charlie and me and we had dinner. Afterward we sat there talking, and before I knew it it was three o'clock in the morning. That night I learned a lot about Lisa Miller. She was born in Long Beach, California, and her parents were divorced when she was a very little girl. Her mother, Imogene, had reared Lisa and her two older brothers, Graham and Philip.

Lisa was a very smart, well-educated girl. She had graduated from Long Beach Polytechnic High School, gone on to Long Beach City College, then to Pierce College and finished up at UCLA. When I heard that list of credits I felt a little intimidated. The only school I ever went to was PS 22, and I stayed in the fourth grade so long I wound up dating my teacher, Mrs. Hollander.

As we sat there talking it became apparent to me that Lisa had always been in love with show business, and her mother had encouraged her. At a very early age Lisa started taking piano lessons, singing lessons, dancing lessons, acting lessons, etc. She told me her whole childhood had been devoted to taking lessons. In fact, she remembered one time

201

when she was about six years old and she watched a little neighbor boy climbing a tree. He went up the tree, swinging from one branch to another like a squirrel, and when he came down Lisa went up to him and asked, "I never saw anything like that! Who do you take your climbing lessons from?"

By the time she was sixteen Lisa thought she knew everything there was to know about show business. And like most young people she had lots of ambitions and very little patience. She fully expected to be a superstar by the time she was seventeen—and by the time she was eighteen at least a living legend. Well, the moment of truth arrived when she learned that the Long Beach Civic Light Opera Association was auditioning for their production of *Funny Girl*. Lisa went right to work. She learned all of Fanny Brice's songs and all of her dialogue, and when she went to the audition they hired her—to play the part of a maid! During a party scene in the second act she came on with one line: "Would anyone care for some oyster dip?"

Lisa's mother came opening night to watch the "living legend," and Lisa told me that after the show her mother was waiting for her when she got home. She hit her with a line Lisa never forgot. As soon as Lisa walked in the door her mother said, "Thirteen years of lessons and you wind up passing the oyster dip!"

Well, that did it for Lisa. She retired from show business, switched her major at UCLA to economics, and decided to become a teacher. And you know, I think the kids would have loved her. She could do a split, kick the back of her head, and teach the multiplication tables to the tune of "Maple Leaf Rag."

Naturally I wondered how she got sidetracked from a teaching career and wound up with a singing group in Las Vegas. Well, here's what she told me, and if the story sounds familiar, I'm sure it must have happened to Ruby Keeler in one of those Warner Bros. musicals.

Auditions were being held for a new singing group called

The Kids Next Door, and Lisa's best friend, Cathy, was going down to try out. Lisa was helping Cathy out by playing the piano for her while she rehearsed. Well, the day of the auditions came, and Cathy was a nervous wreck. She was ready to give the whole thing up until Lisa agreed to go to the audition with her for moral support. When they got to the auditorium there were about thirty or forty kids who were being called up one at a time to audition. As it got closer to Cathy's turn she became more and more nervous. Finally she panicked, shoved her music into Lisa's hands, and ran out the door. Just then the man in charge pointed to Lisa and said, "You're next!" She went over to the man, but before she could explain about Cathy he took the music, the piano player started to play, and before Lisa knew it she was singing. That same afternoon she signed a contract with The Kids Next Door and retired from becoming a teacher.

But that's not the end of the story. Two weeks later Lisa was playing Las Vegas, and Cathy was teaching school. Wouldn't Ruby Keeler have loved that story? And Joan Blondell would have been perfect as Cathy.

Well, that three o'clock session with Lisa was the beginning. I had three more weeks at the Riviera, and during that time I saw Lisa practically every night. She was an absolute joy to be with, and we had a marvelous time together. Now, you may wonder how a man of seventy-two and a girl of eighteen could have anything in common. I can't really explain it, but there was something there that made it work. Part of it was she made me feel young. She treated me like I was one of The Kids Next Door. After a week with Lisa she almost had me convinced that I was twenty years old. I was ready to go out and buy a long-haired toupée and rent some pimples.

When the engagement ended at the Riviera, Lisa went on tour with The Kids and I went back home to Beverly Hills. After I'd been home for several days I just didn't feel right; I was restless and bored. Finally I figured out what it was; I wanted to hear "The Maple Leaf Rag" again. About three weeks later I was sitting at home when the phone rang. I picked it up and a voice said, "If you're going to be home tonight, I'd like to bring over some oyster dip."

Lisa was back!

We picked up right where we left off in Las Vegas, and it was just as much fun here as it was there. It wasn't long before I realized that this little girl was filling a need that was missing at this particular time in my life. I always felt very comfortable when I was with Lisa, because there was never any problem about the difference in our ages. Now, when some older men take out a young girl they get very self-conscious; like my friend George Pallay who introduces his young dates as his nieces, or the type who takes his date to some out-of-the-way place and sits at a table in a dark corner so nobody should see them. It was never that way with Lisa and me. Whenever I took her out to dinner we always went to places where my friends were, and we didn't sit in some dark corner, we sat at a front table with the lights up.

One night at Chasen's I kiddingly said to Lisa, "I get a feeling that some of the people in this room might think you're a little too young for me."

Without batting an eye she said, "You're wrong, you're too young for me. As soon as I find an older man I'm leaving you." That didn't bother me; I knew there weren't any older men.

One night after we had been seeing each other for about two months, we were watching television together, and I said, "Lisa, you've told me so much about your family, I'd like to meet them. Why don't I have them all over here to dinner some night."

She didn't even answer me. She jumped up, made three phone calls, came back, and said, "They'll all be here Saturday."

That night I had a little trouble getting to sleep. I kept saying to myself, "What are you getting yourself into? Ever

204

her mother is too young for you! All of them will probably hate you. You must be out of your mind!" I went on talking to myself like that all night. I said some pretty funny things, but I was too worried to enjoy them.

Well, Saturday night came, and so did the Miller family. When I met Lisa's mother, Imogene, I couldn't get over it. She looked and acted exactly like an older version of Lisa. She was a charming woman, and I felt right at home with her the moment I met her.

And I knew I was going to like Lisa's brother, Philip, because he brought along his guitar. She must have told him I was a singer. He was a schoolteacher, and his lovely wife, Andi, was planning to enter college to study law.

Lisa's other brother, Graham, was a former All-American football player; 6'2", 240 pounds, and all muscle. When he went to shake my hand I pulled it back; I didn't want to hurt the kid. He was working in a brokerage house, and Laurel, his very pretty wife, was a speech therapist.

Well, I said hello to everybody, and that's the last thing I said for the next three hours. When the Miller clan gets together they don't need anybody else. I was all prepared to make a good impression on the family; I had about twenty-five minutes of my real funny anecdotes worked out, but I never got a chance to use them. I sat there while they told stories, laughed, kidded each other, and had a marvelous time. This went on all through dinner. Then, afterward, they all trooped into the living room and Lisa's mother played the piano, Philip played his guitar, and the rest of the Millers sang and danced. I just sat there with a mouthful of anecdotes. I couldn't believe this family. Just before they left, Imogene started playing "The Maple Leaf Rag" and everybody else lined up and went into a time step. Then they did an off-to-Buffalo and finished with a brake. After they left I was in a daze—this wasn't a family, this was a Fanchon & Marco unit.

The next time I saw Lisa she told me her family had had a

marvelous time at my house. She said, "G.B., my family all loved you." (Oh, I forgot to tell you, she always called me G.B.) Then, with that pixie smile of hers, she added, "But they were sort of surprised, they wondered why a man who'd been in show business as long as you have didn't get up and do something."

Shortly after this I was booked to play three weeks at the Frontier Hotel in Las Vegas, so I got an idea. Lisa was a talented girl, so I put together a little routine in which we talked and danced and sang and worked it into my act. We did it in Las Vegas, and the routine was a hit. Lisa was not only good in the act, but she was great company to have around. At the risk of hurting Charlie Reade's feelings, a man gets tired of looking at his road manager twenty-four hours a day.

Well, after the Frontier we played the Palmer House in Chicago, we did two television shows with Bob Hope, one with Jackie Gleason, and another with Dean Martin. Then we went to London and appeared on *The Max Bygraves Show*. While we were in London, one day we decided to visit Westminster Abbey. When our cab pulled up front I got out one side and Lisa got out the other. Now, English money has always been hard for me to figure out, so it took me some time to pay the driver. After the cab pulled away I looked around, but there was no Lisa. I thought she must have gone in ahead of me, so I went into the Abbey to look for her. What I didn't know was that she had gone into a nearby shop to price something.

When I got inside the Abbey it was breathtaking. There was a reverent quietness about it that was overwhelming. There were a number of people there tiptoeing around looking at this impressive display of England's history, and if anyone so much as cleared his throat it reverberated from wall to wall. When my eyes became accustomed to the dim light I quietly moved around looking for Lisa. Suddenly the stillness was shattered with the loudest stage whisper I ever heard: "G.B., ARE YOU IN THERE?" I went into a state of shock as those words echoed all over the Abbey. I sneaked out as fast as I could, and when I found Lisa out front I grabbed her by the arm and started looking for a taxi.

"G.B.," she protested, "we came to see Westminster Abbey!"

"Some other time, Lisa," I muttered. About then a cab came up, and as we got in I said, "I only hope the people in there thought that G.B. stood for Great Britain."

A few months after we returned from London Lisa moved into my house. Now hold it, I know what you're thinking! I admit I was thinking the same thing, but it didn't happen that way. It all started with Lisa's mother, Imogene. She had been going with a very nice man named Lee White, and several times I had both of them to dinner at my house. Well, one day I got a phone call from Imogene asking me if she could come by the house and see me alone that afternoon, it was important. It turned out that Lee had asked her to marry him, but she didn't know what to do.

I said, "Well, Imogene, the first thing is, do you love Lee?"

"I love him very much," she answered, "but I'm worried about Lisa. If I marry Lee, I'll have to move up north to Ukiah because his business is there. I just can't stand the thought of leaving my baby all alone in that big house in Long Beach."

Well, this sort of amused me. I said, "Your baby? Imogene, your baby Lisa can not only take care of herself, she can take care of me, you, Lee, her two brothers, and their wives—and if Kissinger has a problem, she can straighten that out, too."

Imogene laughed and said, "G.B., you said exactly what I hoped you'd say. You've really taken a load off my shoulders."

Well, we had a martini and toasted her coming marriage,

which took place two weeks later. The newlyweds moved to Ukiah, and the "Baby" was left alone in that big house in Long Beach.

After that, when Lisa and I had a date and got in late, instead of taking that long drive to Long Beach she'd stay over at my place. I have a rather large home, and upstairs there's an extra suite that my children used to live in when they were growing up. When Lisa stayed over I'd have Arlette and Daniel make it ready for her. This arrangement worked out fine for everybody.

On one of the nights when she didn't stay over we had an early dinner, watched a little television, and Lisa drove home to Long Beach. Well, at two o'clock that morning my phone rang and it was Lisa. She was crying, and when I asked her what the trouble was she sobbed into the phone, "G.B., my ting-a-ling is missing!"

I wasn't quite awake, but *that* woke me up. I had no idea what a ting-a-ling was, but I was hoping it wasn't what I thought. Anyway, trying to calm her down, I said, "Look, Lisa, I'll have Daniel and Arlette look around, and if you left your ting-a-ling here, you can pick it up tomorrow."

"Oh, G.B.," she wailed, "this is serious. I left the window open and it got out!"

"Lisa," I said, "calm down. Now—what got out?"

She said, "Ting-a-Ling, my cat!"

Well, this was a pretty dull finish, but she was genuinely worried, so I said, "Just leave the window open, and I'm sure Ting-a-Ling will come back." And he did. When it comes to a crisis I always know how to handle it.

One night things came to a head. Lisa and I had been to a movie and we were sitting having a nightcap and watching Johnny Carson. After a few minutes Lisa got up and turned off the television. Looking very serious, she sat down beside me on the couch and said, "G.B., I think it's time we discussed something very important."

I said, "Well, it must be important, you just turned off an interview between Johnny Carson and Lyle Talbot."

Instead of a laugh all I got from her was a weary sigh, and then she continued. "Please, G.B., I really mean it. I hate being alone in that big house down in Long Beach—and since I spend half my time here anyway—why couldn't I just move in?"

The same thing had crossed my mind, but I did have certain reservations. "Lisa," I said, "it's all right with me, but aren't you worried about what people will think?"

She said, "No. If you're not worried, and I'm not worried, let people think what they want and let them worry."

"Then it's settled," I said. "You can move in tomorrow."

She took me by the hand and said, "Come upstairs, G.B., I want to show you something." Well, we walked into the suite she used, and there hanging in the closet was her entire wardrobe; her slippers were under the bed, her toothbrush was hanging by the washbasin, and all her luggage was there. She gave me a big innocent smile and said, "I'm so glad you said I could move in, G.B., now I won't have to move out."

Now, that's the story of how and why Lisa moved into my house. You must admit that it's a very believable story. In fact, I just read it over and I'm beginning to believe it myself.

During the time that Lisa lived at my house we had a lot of wonderful times together, but that doesn't mean each of us didn't have a life of his own. Lisa had her circle of young friends she went out with, and I still went to the club and enjoyed the company of my friends. Of course, her life was a little more exciting than mine, because my youngest friend was Georgie Jessel. It was a perfect arrangement for both of us.

Along about then Lisa decided to continue her education and retired again from show business. Maybe I should say semiretired, because she was still interested in the theater. She enrolled in Immaculate Heart College where she eventually received her Bachelor of Arts degree in Theater and English. It was while attending Immaculate Heart that she came home one evening with a friend of hers whom she introduced as Albin Konopka. Albin was a promising young pianist and seemed to be a very nice young man. I didn't realize it at the time, but this was the beginning of the story of how Lisa moved out of my house.

Now, moving out didn't take as long as moving in. It was only a week or two after I had met Albin that Lisa turned off Johnny Carson again and sat down next to me on the couch. This time she said, "G.B., I'm in love with Albin, and we plan to be married."

For a minute I panicked; I thought Albin was going to move in, too. But I realized she was serious, so I said to her, "Lisa, this is a very important step in your life, have you talked it over with your mother?"

"Oh, yes," she answered, "I talked to her on the phone this morning, and she said 'If it's all right with G.B., it's all right with me.'"

I gave her a little hug and said, "Anything that makes you happy, kid, is okay with me." So she and Albin set the date for their marriage.

The wedding was a lovely affair. It took place in a very picturesque setting, high in the Palos Verdes Hills, overlooking the ocean. There were about one hundred and fifty relatives and friends there. After the ceremony, when I danced with Lisa, I said, "Lisa, I've never seen you look happier."

She said, "I am. It's because I'm in love with Albin." Then, after a pause, she smiled at me and added, "G.B., you'll always be the best friend I've ever had."

The following day the bride and groom moved to New York, where Albin had a scholarship at the Juilliard School of Music. Subsequently they moved to Paris, where they live at the time this is being written. Albin has developed into a very accomplished concert pianist, and is continuing his studies with Mademoiselle Nadia Boulanger, an internationally famous music instructor. I hear from Lisa frequently, and both she and Albin are very happy. When they return to the United States I'm sure Albin will be giving concerts, and Lisa will be able to play "The Maple Leaf Rag" in French.

When Lisa got married I don't want you to get the idea that I didn't miss her. I did—a great deal. There was a very special affection between Lisa and me, and there always will be. This had been a very enjoyable interlude in my life, but as I've said before in this book, I believe you've just got to take life as it comes. In the words of one of our foremost philosophers, Doris Day—"*Que será, será!*"

The Sunshine Boys

We all know that Neil Simon wrote a hit play called *The Sunshine Boys*, and we all know that Neil Simon wrote a hit movie called *The Sunshine Boys*. And since he did so well with that title, I don't see why I shouldn't have a chapter called *The Sunshine Boys*, so that's why this chapter is called—The Sunshine Boys. I don't say it's going to be a hit, but then again I'm not Neil Simon.

Now that I started off with a little laugh—a very little one—I'd like to get serious for a moment. As I said at the beginning of this book, I don't believe anybody should retire, no matter what his or her age is. In fact, that thought is so important I'm going to repeat it again—*I don't believe anybody should retire, no matter what his or her age is!* And I'm living proof of this point. Well, not completely living; I must admit that every Tuesday at five minutes after one I cough a little.

Now, you all know that I've spent my entire life in show business, then at the age of seventy-nine I made one movie, *The Sunshine Boys*, and it's like I'm just getting started. That should be an example to everyone. I didn't quit, I stayed in there, and I finally got so old that I became new again.

Playing the part of Al Lewis in *The Sunshine Boys* was the most exciting thing that ever happened to me. Let me tell you how it all came about. Originally in 1974 Jack Benny was signed to play the part of Al Lewis, and Ray Stark, the producer, was testing other well-known vaudeville comedians to play opposite Jack in the role of Willie Clark. Well, on August 7 of that year I received a script from Ray with a note asking me to look over the part of Willie. I knew I was wrong for the part, but it didn't make any difference, because on August 9 I was in Cedars of Lebanon Hospital having open-heart surgery. I was wrong for that part, too, but I figured I better not turn it down or I might be making a quick exit.

Fortunately I had a very rapid recovery period, and by the time I was back on my feet, Walter Matthau had been cast to play opposite Jack in the picture. I was very glad for both of them because I knew they'd make a marvelous team.

Then Fate took a cruel twist. Jack Benny became very ill, and in a matter of a few weeks he was gone. This was one of the low points of my life. My best friend was gone, careerwise I wasn't in great demand, and I wasn't getting any younger. To some people this might be the time to throw in the towel, but that's not the way I think. I truly do believe that if you can't do anything about a bad situation, you've got to learn to live with it. So I continued my habit of coming into the office each morning and meeting with Packy and Jack Langdon. I wasn't booked anyplace and we had nothing to do, so we just sat around writing funny routines. And it's hard to know whether a routine is funny or not when you've got no place to play it.

One day we were sitting around the office playing with our pencils when my manager, Irving Fein, came in. He seemed unusually ill at ease, and after a bit of small talk he got to the point. He said, "George, how would you feel about playing the part of Al Lewis in *The Sunshine Boys*?"

I was stunned. For a moment I didn't know what to say. "Irving, I don't think I should do it. That was Jack's part, and if I played it, I just wouldn't feel right."

"George, I think I can help you," Irving said. "I was Jack's manager for twenty-six years, and nobody knew the man any better than I did. Take my word for it, nothing would make Jack happier than to have you do that part."

I still didn't know what to say. Irving turned to Packy and Jack Langdon and said, "Boys, what do you think?" They both enthusiastically agreed it was a marvelous idea. But in spite of all this encouragement I still had reservations. I said, "Irving, give me a chance to think it over."

Irving opened his briefcase and pulled out a copy of the script of *The Sunshine Boys*. "Good. And while you're thinking it over tonight read this script and call me in the morning."

Well, that night I read the script and all of my doubts vanished. It was a beautiful script, and I fell in love with every word. It was like everything Al Lewis said came out of my mouth. I didn't even wait until morning. I called Irving that night. When he picked up the phone I said, "Irving, this is Al Lewis speaking."

He laughed and said, "George, I knew this would happen. I've arranged for you to read for Neil Simon and Herb Ross at ten o'clock Thursday morning."

Well, for the next three days I buried my head in that script, and when Thursday came around I not only knew my part, I knew everybody else's part. I wasn't a bit nervous about reading that morning, because the character of Al Lewis fit me like a glove. Al Lewis was supposed to be born in New York, he was a vaudevillian, he was old, and he was Jewish. Well, I was born in New York, I was a vaudevillian, I was old . . . but how they found out I was Jewish I'll never know. They must have seen me in the locker room at Hillcrest.

At ten o'clock I read for Neil Simon and Herb Ross, who was directing the picture. They must have liked me because when I finished and started to hand the script to Herb, he said, "You keep it, George, I think you're going to be needing it."

Well, the next few days were very nervous ones for me,

wondering whether I had the part or not. But I didn't hear a word. Then one day the trade papers, *Variety* and the *Hollywood Reporter* came out saying that I was set for *The Sunshine Boys*.

But nobody called me and said, "George, you've got the part!"

A couple of days later I received a beautiful leather script-holder from Ray Stark. On the cover embossed in gold letters was THE SUNSHINE BOYS and my name.

But nobody said, "George, you've got the part!"

Next I was invited to a luncheon at MGM in the private executive dining room. There were six of us: Frank Rosenfelt, president of MGM; Dan Melnick, vice-president in charge of production; Walter Matthau; Herb Ross; Irving Fein, and myself. It was a delightful luncheon. We laughed and talked, told anecdotes, the food was delicious, and everybody was very friendly. When we broke up, Herb Ross said to Walter Matthau, "Come on, Walter, let's go downstairs and pick out your wardrobe for *The Sunshine Boys*." Then Frank Rosenfelt shook hands with me, and Dan Melnick shook hands with me.

But nobody said, "George, you've got the part!"

By now two weeks had passed. When the phone rang again, it was Irving Fein. He told me MGM wanted me to go see their doctor for an insurance examination. Well, I'd gone this far, so I figured why not. The next day I went to the doctor's office, and he turned out to be a young doctor, about forty years old. He got right down to business and put me through all the preliminary examinations. They turned out fine. Then he got very serious. "Mr. Burns," he said, "I happen to know that five months ago you had open-heart surgery, and now to complete this examination I have to give you an electrocardiogram to test your heart."

I could see he was a little tense, so I thought I'd soften up the situation. I said, "Doctor, go ahead, that's what I'm here for. And if I enjoy it, let's do it every Monday."

216

He was not amused. Very slowly he explained, "Before I give you this test you've got to walk on this treadmill. Now it's uphill, you've got to walk for two minutes, and it's very strenuous. Do you think it will be too much for you?"

"Doctor," I said, "Neil Simon is a great writer, I read the script and I love my part—start the treadmill."

Before he turned it on he cautioned me, "Now, Mr. Burns, when you're on the treadmill, if you feel the least bit of pain, or dizziness, or get short of breath—anything at all—tell me immediately and I'll stop the machine."

Well, he started the treadmill, I got on it and started to walk. He stood right next to me and never took his eyes off me. Every five seconds he'd say, "How do you feel?" . . . "How do you feel?" . . . "How do you feel?" And I'd answer, "Fine!" . . . "Fine!" . . . Fine!" This went on for two minutes, and when I got off the machine I felt great. Then I took a look at the doctor. He was white as a sheet, trembling all over, and wringing wet. I said, "Doctor, did you ever have open-heart surgery?"

He said, "No."

I said, "Well, you ought to have it, you look bad."

The following morning I got the results of my tests and everything came out perfect. But still—

Nobody said, "George, you've got the part!"

Well, for three more days we sat around the office and heard nothing. Finally, I said to Packy and Jack, "Fellows, it doesn't look good. I've done everything they asked me to do, so I guess we might as well forget about it and start playing with our pencils again." Wouldn't you know, the phone rang. I knew who it was. I picked up the phone and said, "Hello, Irving."

Irving said, "George, the picture starts Monday. They want you to be on Stage 28 at nine o'clock to start rehearsals."

Do you know, that was almost two years ago? I made the picture, it turned out to be a big hit, I traveled all over the world to promote it, and I won an Academy Award for Best Supporting Actor. Would you believe that to this day nobody has ever said—

"George, you got the part!"

During my many years in show business with Gracie, whether it was vaudeville, radio, television, or movies we were always Burns and Allen, and I played George Burns. Now here I was playing the part of Al Lewis in *The Sunshine Boys*, and it was a brand-new experience for me. But, as I said, I felt the character of Al Lewis so strongly I could hardly wait to get to the studio that Monday morning. At the time I said to myself, "If I'm a hit as Al Lewis, I might never go back to being George Burns again. I'll let somebody with less talent play him."

For the first two or three days the cast sat around a table and read the script to get familiar with it. Now, one of the actors was a method actor who needed a motivation for everything he did. He wouldn't make a move unless he knew why he was making it. There was a scene in the script that called for him to go to the bathroom, and he said to the director, Herb Ross, "*Why* am I going to the bathroom?"

Herb said, "*Why?* Who knows?—for the same reason that everybody goes to the bathroom."

"I know that, but *why?*"

Herb just looked at him. "Well, maybe in the scene before that you had breakfast."

"Did I have a big breakfast, or did I have a small breakfast?"

Herb's eyes narrowed a bit. "What difference does that make?"

"I want to know how long to stay in the bathroom."

Herb thought a second, then he said, "I just decided you're not going to use the bathroom."

"*Why* am I not going to use the bathroom?"

Very calmly and quietly Herb answered, "You won't be able to get in. The actor who's taking your place will be using it."

That was the end of the method actor. And from then on I didn't take any chances. Whenever Herb Ross looked at me I went to the bathroom!

By the end of the first week something happened that proved to me that no matter how long you're in this business you're never really sure of yourself. By now we were on our feet walking through the scenes, and every day when we broke for lunch Neil Simon and Herb Ross would come to the commissary and eat with us. However, this one day I heard Herb say to Neil, "I've ordered lunch for us in my office. We've got a problem and we have to make a decision today."

When I heard this I got an awful sinking feeling. I'd seen what had happened to the method actor, and for some reason I figured I was next. It looked like I was going back to being George Burns again. Well, I couldn't eat a bite of my lunch. My new movie career was ending before it started. All sorts of thoughts went through my head and I was absolutely miserable. When I got back to the set I noticed Herb and Neil sitting with their heads together. I knew it would be embarrassing for them to tell me they were letting me go, so I thought I'd make it easier for them and bow out gracefully. I went over to them and said, "Gentlemen, I know what your problem is, and I'm going to solve it for you."

They both gave me a blank look, then they looked at each other, and Herb said to me, "We just decided during lunch to change the ending of the picture, how would you know that?"

Well, it was my turn to look blank. I realized I had let my imagination run away with me, but I didn't want them to know it. I said, "Fellows, I'm glad to hear that because I felt the picture needed a new ending, too!" And without waiting for their reaction I ran into my dressing room and ordered lunch.

Finally the day came when they were going to shoot my first scene. I had a very early call, and while I was driving to

219

the studio I remembered something that Edward G. Robinson once told me. He had said that in every picture he ever made, before they shot the first scene if he got nervous, he knew he was going to give a good performance. This kind of worried me, because in one hour I was going to shoot my first scene and I wasn't a bit nervous. But then I figured it would happen when I got to my dressing room. Well, I got to my dressing room and sat down and waited. I must have sat there four or five minutes. Nothing happened. I almost fell asleep. I thought maybe if I started putting on my wardrobe that would do it. While I was dressing I began talking to myself. "George, remember what Eddie said—if you want to give a good performance, you've got to get nervous." Did you ever try to make yourself get nervous? Get butterflies in your stomach? Make your palms sweat? You can't do it. In fact, I almost got nervous because I wasn't getting nervous.

When I finished dressing I stood in front of the mirror and I forgot all about being nervous. I couldn't get over the way I looked. I had on a dark pin-striped suit, a polka-dot bow tie, and a white silk scarf. Over that I wore a blue top coat with a black velvet collar and, to top it all, a black felt fedora hat and a heavy cane with a gold top and gloves. I stared at myself for a minute, but it wasn't what I expected. I didn't look like Spencer Tracy, or Jimmy Cagney, or Paul Muni, or Marlon Brando—I didn't even look like an actor. I looked like an honorary pallbearer.

Then I looked at myself from different angles; first from the left, then from the right, then straight ahead. Then I threw back my head and laughed; then I looked down and frowned, but something was missing. Finally I realized what it was—no cigar. Even with all those clothes on I felt naked. And there wasn't going to be any cigar, because Neil and Herb had decided I wasn't going to smoke in the picture. I couldn't imagine myself without a cigar. It would be the first time I ever worked alone.

Well, the big moment arrived for me to start my new ca

eer as an actor. They called for me, and I walked onto the set with no cigar, no butterflies, and dry palms. Now, my first scene was with Richard Benjamin. I knock on the door, and he opens it. When he sees me he says, "Hello, Mr. Lewis, come on in." Well, when he opened the door and said, "Hello, Mr. Lewis, come on in," I just looked around. I didn't know whom he was talking to. When I heard the name Lewis I thought maybe Jerry got the part.

Well, Herb stopped the scene and came over to me and said, "George, you're Mr. Lewis." I felt better right away. I knew if I couldn't remember that my name was Lewis, I was nervous enough to give a good performance. Well, after that there was no problem. Dick Benjamin and I went through the whole scene, and Herb Ross loved it.

Now, I'll let you in on a little secret. I found out that acting is easy. It's much easier to be an actor than it is to walk out on the stage by yourself and tell jokes and sing for an hour. On the stage if it's no good, that's it, you don't have a chance to do it over, but when you're acting in a movie and it's no good, you do it over and over and over until you get it right. And when you're on the stage you're all by yourself, you don't have Walter Matthau on one side and Richard Benjamin on the other to help you.

Another great thing I discovered about acting is that you don't have to stand on your feet all the time. Ninety percent of the time you're sitting down. At this stage of the game if I can sit down and get paid for doing it, I'm in the right business. Makes me wonder why I've been standing up all these years.

Now, let me tell you what I meant about acting being easy. To be a good actor all you have to do is listen. In that first scene when Dick Benjamin opened the door and said to me, "Hello, Mr. Lewis, come on in," I went in. Now, that's good acting! If I had stayed out in the hall, that's bad acting. When I got inside, Dick Benjamin said, "How do you feel, Mr. Lewis?" And I said, "Fine, thank you." Again, that's good acting! Now, when he said, "How do you feel, Mr.

Lewis," if I had said, "Look on the floor, maybe it fell down," that's bad acting. That means you're not listening. And to be a great actor you've got to listen. So when I said, "Fine, thank you," that meant I was listening. I was listening so hard that in my next picture I might even ask for more money.

I had always heard that the toughest thing about acting was to be able to laugh and to be able to cry. I say nonsense! If I'm doing a scene in which I'm supposed to cry, all I do is think of my sex life. If I'm doing a scene in which I'm supposed to laugh, all I do is think of my sex life. I must really be a hell of an actor. This morning after taking a shower I looked at myself in the mirror and laughed and cried at the same time.

There are those who say that the most difficult emotion to portray on the screen is pain. Again, I say nonsense! If a scene calls for me to register extreme pain, it's simple. All I do is wear tight jockey shorts.

That sums up my formula for being a good actor. Of course, there are other schools of thought on the subject, but everyone must decide which works best for him. As Harry Fink of "Fink's Mules" once said, "Every mule has his own personality." Personally, I don't know what that means, but Harry Fink went around saying things like that.

But I've been serious long enough. Back to *The Sunshine Boys.* I never had such kid-glove treatment in my life as I did during the shooting of that picture. The producer, the director, the assistants, the crew, the cameraman, the makeup man, they all treated me as though I were a china doll. They acted as though any minute I might break into little pieces. I suppose they were nervous because Jack Benny had passed away, and I had had open-heart surgery five months before. I don't know if they were worried about me personally; they probably just wanted to make sure I lasted until the picture was finished.

If I so much as mentioned a cup of tea, before I could

move there'd be four cups of tea in front of me. If I sneezed, before anybody could say "Gesundheit!" I was surrounded by Kleenex. And everywhere I went somebody was following me with a chair. They'd say, "Sit down, Mr. Burns. . . ." "Take it easy, Mr. Burns. . . ." "Rest, Mr. Burns. . . ." I got so tired of sitting down whenever I wanted to stand up I'd have to sneak into the men's room. One day the property man even followed me in there. I said, "Please, this is one thing I like to do by myself."

I didn't wear any makeup in the picture, but they hired Dick Smith, one of the top makeup men in the business, for Walter. Walter is only in his mid-fifties, but they had to make him look as old as I did. It took Dick two hours to put on Walter's makeup. He had to shave part of his head to make him look bald, he put wrinkles in his face and neck, and even protruding veins on the back of his hands. It was a tremendous makeup job, and Dick Smith is very expensive. I'm not sure, but I think he got more money for making up Walter than I got for making the picture.

Now, when Walter arrived in the morning, he had a lively bounce in his walk, and he used to do little dance steps while he was singing or whistling; he was full of life. To show you what a complete actor Walter Matthau is, when he got up from that makeup table he not only looked like an old man, he *was* an old man. His whole body slumped, his shoulders sagged, his clothes hung on him, and when he walked he dragged his feet. The first day I saw him shuffle onto the set I jumped up and gave him my chair. After I helped him down, he looked up and said, "Thanks, son."

I don't hesitate to say that *The Sunshine Boys* was a fine picture. Everyone involved with the picture enjoyed making it, and nobody was ever late for work in the morning. All of the pieces seemed to fit, and the man who put them together was Herb Ross, the director. He was a tremendous help to me, and he got the most out of everybody without even raising his voice.

Let me give you an example of how Herb worked. In this one particular scene he thought I was playing it too serious, but he didn't say a word to me. Between takes he went to Walter and quietly told him he thought I was a little tight in this scene and asked Walter to do something to loosen me up. Well, that's all he had to say to Walter. Now, this scene was a single shot of me, and Walter was standing behind the camera feeding me lines. Herb called for action so we started doing the scene. Right in the middle of it Walter dropped his pants. I'm sure it must have loosened me up a little, but I never lost my concentration. I went right on with the scene and, believe me, it's not easy to look a man in the eye when he's standing there with his pants down. I admit when the scene was over I did take a little peek. Walter's eyes are prettier.

Anyway, Herb liked the scene, so Walter pulled his pants up and we went on with the picture. By using a little psychology Herb got the job done, and he didn't even have to raise his voice. All he had to do was lower Walter's pants.

Another thing I learned is that acting in a movie is entirely different than appearing on the stage in front of an audience. On the stage I'm very conscious of the audience because I need them. If I look out there and see them laughing and enjoying what I'm doing, it's like having a love affair with them. But in a movie it's just the opposite. The only audience you have is the crew, and they can't make a sound. No matter how funny the scene might be, they don't dare let out a snicker. When Walter and I would do a funny scene we knew where the laughs should be, but there was nothing but silence. He was used to this, but for me it felt strange; no reaction, no laughs, no applause—I felt like I was playing Altoona again.

This is where concentration is important. You know there are fifty or sixty people gathered around you so close you can practically touch them, but you have to block them out completely. Your concentration has to be so strong that you don't even know there's a camera there. I worked so hard at concentrating I even took it home with me. One night when I arrived home Daniel opened the door for me. I said, "Why are you opening the door? Where's Daniel?"

Daniel said, "Mr. Burns, I'm Daniel."

"Excuse me," I said, "I thought you were Dick Benjamin."

Now, you know the above story is true. George Burns might lie a little, but not Al Lewis.

Well, after we wrapped up our scenes here at MGM, the company went on location to New York City for five weeks. We shot several scenes in the lobby of the Ansonia Hotel. Now, the Ansonia Hotel has been around as long as New York has been around. At the turn of the century it was a very elegant hotel where all the famous opera stars used to stay. On the second day of shooting the manager of the Ansonia brought out an old registration book he had in his office and proudly opened it up and showed me some of the people who had registered there. There were Enrico Caruso, John McCormack, Mary Garden, and Jenny Lind. Then he said, "Mr. Burns, wouldn't you like to sign your name in the book?" I was happy to, so I did. It was exciting having my name there on the same page with four other great singers.

But the highlight of the trip was when the Friars Club in New York gave Walter and me a testimonial dinner. It was a big affair, and practically all of Walter's speech was about me. He said I was the most natural actor he ever worked with, and every day he was learning something new from me. Then he went on to say what a joy I was to work with, and it was such a pleasure to be around me that he couldn't wait to leave home and come to work in the morning.

I was sitting on the dais next to Walter's wife, Carole. Right about then I felt a little nudge in my ribs. Carole leaned over and whispered into my ear, "George, I'm afraid I've got a problem. I think my husband is in love with his leading man."

I whispered back, "Your husband is the one who has the problem. I think I'm in love with his wife."

But everywhere we went, if there was an interview, Walter kept saying these flattering things about me. It got to be embarrassing. I mean, it would have been embarrassing if they weren't true.

(Here's a little footnote that I'm too tired to put at the bottom of the page. Packy and Jack said that line about me not being embarrassed makes me sound conceited. But I don't care, at my age I haven't got time to be humble.)

Whenever I'm in New York I always manage to spend some time with my friends Jesse Block and his wife, Eva. I've known Jesse and Eva since the old vaudeville days when they did a great man and woman act, and they were billed as "Block and Sully." Jesse has been a member of the Friars Club as long as I have, and one day we were having lunch there. Some of the scenes for *The Sunshine Boy* were being shot there at the club, and it so happened that wasn't in any of them. Jesse couldn't understand that. He said to me, "George, you've been a member of the Friar Club practically all your life. It doesn't seem right that you're not doing a scene here at the club. Why don't you tell Neil Simon to write one for you?"

Jesse seemed to have the notion that all I had to do was snap my fingers and Neil Simon would rush to his typewriter. I didn't want to embarrass him, so I said, "Jesse, it's a great idea, I'll ask him."

Well, that didn't stop Jesse. He said, "George, in the scene I'm sure you'll be working with somebody, so why don't you have Neil write me in."

I said, "Jesse, that's a great idea, I'll ask him."

He went right on. "And as long as he's writing me in, why don't you have him write a few lines for Eva?"

I said, "Jesse, that's a great idea, I'll ask him."

By now Jesse was all excited. He said, "George, do you think he'll do it?"

I said, "Jesse, I'll let you know as soon as Neil Simon throws me out of his office."

Well, a week later was the last day of the picture. Now, when you wind up shooting on a picture that ran as smoothly as *The Sunshine Boys*, you can't help but have mixed emotions. On one hand you're happy it's finished, and on the other you wish you were just starting again. When Herb Ross said, "That's it, boys, wrap it up!" nobody wanted to leave the set. I looked over at Walter Matthau, who was slumped down in a chair. He had on that old-man makeup and really looked tired. Ray Stark was on the set that day, so I pointed to Walter and said, "Ray, there's one thing I'll never understand. How did you talk the insurance company into letting a man that age make this picture?"

Although the actual filming of the picture was finished, another phase of the operation was just beginning. Dick Kahn, vice-president in charge of MGM's publicity and advertising department, and the United Artists publicity gang outlined an intensive campaign for Walter and myself to publicize the film. They worked in conjunction with my personal public relations people, Steinberg, Lipsman, and Brokaw. This involved countless magazine and newspaper interviews and appearances on talk shows from coast to coast. All of this was coordinated by one of the brightest and most capable publicists I've ever met. Her name is Regina Gruss, she works for MGM, and she is every bit as nice as she is talented. In spite of the heavy pressures of Regina's job, I never knew her to be rude, lose her temper, or be anything but pleasant through the entire campaign.

Regina had everything worked out on a very tight time schedule. There was one day when I had to give about six interviews. I was stopping at the Sherry-Netherland Hotel in New York, and my first interview was at ten o'clock in the morning. Regina cautioned me I could only give the columnist exactly ten minutes because we had to rush right over to NBC. Well, asking me to do ten minutes is embarrassing. Acrobats do ten minutes. Anyway, the interview was going very well, and I was really rolling. At the end of ten minutes I was right in the middle of my story about how Sid Gary and I put the two live chickens in the icebox, and Regina was getting very nervous. She was standing by the door, holding my hat and coat and making little motions that we had to leave. Well, I certainly wasn't going to stop in the middle of a classic story like the one about the two live chickens in the icebox, so by the time I finished, the interview had lasted about a half hour.

In the taxi on our way to NBC Regina gave me a little lecture. She said, "George, you've upset our schedule for the whole day. In the first place I didn't believe one word of that story about the chickens in the icebox. In fact, I don't believe any of your stories. So from now on you're just going to have to start telling shorter lies."

I let that little statement sink in, then I looked at Regina and said, "Teacher, when we get to NBC do I have time to go to the men's room?"

Regina laughed and said, "All right, George, but try to make it shorter than the chicken story."

My relationship with Regina during the promotion for the picture was perfect. She went with Walter and me for the opening of the picture in Chicago, in London, and even all the way to Australia. And boy, did we need her! I don't think we could have done it without her.

For me, the most exciting opening was when the picture premiered at Radio City Music Hall in New York. Now, my name had been up in lights before, but I felt an extra something special when I saw it on the marquee of Radio City Music Hall. It meant I had made it as an actor. Since New York was my hometown, I'd been to the Music Hall many times, but this night was different—they let me in for free.

All through the making of the movie I hadn't watched any of the rushes or gone to any of the previews. I wanted to see it for the first time in this magnificent theater with an audience. Well, opening night the picture started, and when

228

it came to my first scene, there I was bigger than life—and bald! I was shocked! I never knew I wore a toupee before.

Well, that brings us right up to now. In my lifetime I've been lucky enough to experience a great many personal high points, but I can honestly say that making *The Sunshine Boys* was one of the highest.

Of course, the highest of all was the night I walked onto the stage of the Dorothy Chandler Pavilion and was presented the Academy Award for Best Supporting Actor of 1975. It would be impossible for me to put down on paper my feelings at that moment. At a time when most people are ending their career, there I stood, an eighty-year-old man, just beginning a new one. I think I'm gonna stay in show business!

Epilogue

In closing, I'd like to say I enjoyed writing this book. The last book I wrote was in 1955. That was twenty-one years ago, and I had so much fun doing this one that I think I'll write one every twenty-one years.

Now, since you've read this far you must have a pretty good idea what my life-style is. I've always believed that life is a lot easier if you're able to laugh at yourself. And it's a lot more fun, too. Whenever I do get serious, it doesn't last very long, because I'm always thinking of a humorous finish.

It's well known that I have a tendency to bend the truth a bit, but basically everything in this book is factual. There are many profound truths here, but they're not easy to find unless you read between the lies. I don't presume to tell anyone how to live their life, but there is one thing I am sure of: No matter what age you are—stay active!

In summing up my philosophy I'm reminded of an ancient Law of Physics that was told to me by the parking lot boy at Chasen's restaurant. It made sense. To him—not to me. Anyway, here's what he said:

> Once a body in motion,
> It tends to remain in motion;
> Once a body at rest,
> It tends to remain at rest.

What the kid meant was:

IF YOU DON'T USE IT, YOU'LL LOSE IT!

Things I Forgot to Put in My Book

When I finished writing this book I found out I had a lot of funny anecdotes left over. They were cluttering up my house. I kept stepping on them and tripping over them, and there's nothing messier than a houseful of funny old anecdotes. I called the Goodwill, and they wouldn't take them; I held a garage sale, and nobody showed up. I didn't know what to do with them. But then I got to thinking—I've been getting laughs with these anecdotes all my life, and even though they might be old to me, they're probably brand new to most of you readers. Anyway, here they are. If you think they're funny, laugh at them. If you don't, you can hold your own garage sale.

* * *

This is one of the greatest inside-show-business stories I have ever heard, and it really happened. Wilton LaKye was one of the finest legitimate actors on Broadway, and like all the other big stars of that time, each year he'd play in vaudeville for five or six weeks. He was headlining the Keith Theater in Cincinnati, and on the bill with him was a little dancing act that opened the show. They called themselves Dunbar and Dixon.

After Monday's rehearsal LaKye went into the bar next door to the theater to have a drink. Dunbar and Dixon happened to come in, and when they saw this big star, Wilton LaKye, they almost jumped out of their skins. They went over to their idol, and Dunbar said, "Mr. LaKye, we just wanted to tell you what a thrill it is for us to play on the same bill with you."

LaKye said, "Thank you, boys."

Then Dixon said, "Mr. LaKye, we would deem it an honor if we could buy you a drink."

LaKye said, "I'm sorry, boys, but I'd just as soon drink alone. I just got a wire saying that I lost my mother."

Dixon shook his head sadly and said, "We know just how you feel—our trunk is missing."

* * *

Another story in the same mood involved an act that called themselves The Seven Happy Fitzpatricks. After their father passed away, every year on the anniversary of his death they put an ad in *Variety* which read:

IN FOND MEMORY OF OUR DEAR DEPARTED FATHER,
THE SEVEN HAPPY FITZPATRICKS

* * *

Years ago in Philadelphia there was a hotel called the Hurley House, and all the small-time vaudeville actors used to stop there. The reason most of us stopped there was because of one waitress, a sexy little thing named Fritzi Watkins. Now, when you'd order breakfast, which consisted of doughnuts and coffee, Fritzi would bring it up to your room. And she'd always stay because she *loved* coffee.

Well, one morning I ordered breakfast, and when she brought it up I said, "Fritzi, how about a little coffee?"

She said, "I'd love to."

Naturally I locked the door, I didn't want the coffee to get cold. Well, five minutes later when I was dunking my doughnut there was a knock on the door and it was Hurley the owner of the hotel. He hollered, "Is Fritzi in there?"

I got panicky. I had an adjoining room with a juggler

234

named Al Jacobi, so I knocked on the door, and when he opened it I pushed in Fritzi. I let Hurley in, he looked around and didn't see Fritzi, so he left. Then I knocked on Jacobi's door, but he wouldn't give me back Fritzi. So I phoned downstairs to Hurley and said, "If you're looking for Fritzi, she's next door in Al Jacobi's room."

Hurley came up, knocked on Jacobi's door, Jacobi opened my door and threw back Fritzi. But this story has a sad ending. In the meantime my coffee got cold.

* * *

In Vaudeville taking bows was an art in itself. The number of bows you took at the end of your act was an indication of how successful you were. Many performers had little gimmicks they used to trick the audience into applauding.

Let me start with Eddie Leonard, one of the great song and dance men. He always worked in blackface, and for years Eddie was one of the top headliners. When he was in his sixties, here's the gimmick he used.

After doing his last number he'd take about three bows, and then in sort of a tired voice he'd say, "Folks, old Eddie ain't gonna be with you much longer. This tired old body is comin' to the end of the road. And when I'm up there on that big stage in the sky, these old ears will always hear the applause you folks are givin' me here tonight. This may be old Eddie's last performance. So I love ya all, and good night, and good-bye."

Well, this brought the audience to their feet. They'd cheer, they'd cry, and they'd applaud. Eddie could have taken bows for four days. Oh, by the way, Eddie made that same speech for the next twenty years.

* * *

Herman Timberg was a comedy monologist who also danced and played the violin. This was his gimmick.

At the finish of his act he'd come out, and just as he was about to take his first bow he'd look into the wings as though somebody were calling him. Then he'd walk off-stage as though he were going to find out what they wanted. Well, the audience resented this; they felt that somebody offstage didn't want to give this fine performer a chance to take his bows. So they'd applaud to bring him back.

Timberg would come back out and do the same thing again. And every time he walked offstage the applause got louder. After milking this gimmick for about five or six times he would finally take a legitimate bow. This time the audience would really go wild because they thought they had won. Timberg was a master at this, and it always worked.

* * *

The greatest bow for sustained applause was the one used by a tramp comedian who called himself Bilbo. He was a genius at pantomime, and the audience loved him. And this is how Bilbo finished his act.

On stage he wore oversized yellow shoes with big round-ed toes. When the curtain came down Bilbo would stand in such a position that it would land on the tops of his shoes, leaving the toes extended in front so the audience could still see them. Then a baby spotlight would hit the shoes, and the audience would start to applaud. At this point Bilbo, behind the curtain, would step out of his shoes and go around and stand in the wings. Now, as long as the spotlight stayed on his shoes the audience kept applauding. Depending on his mood, when Bilbo thought the applause had gone on long enough he'd step onstage in his stocking feet and take a bow. The audience realized they had been fooled and they loved him for it.

Unfortunately, this story also has a sad ending. Bilbo was finally booked into Hammerstein's on 42nd Street and Broadway, which was the Palace Theater of the time. He

236

opened on a Monday and was never better. But what the audience didn't know was that Bilbo had a heart condition. At the end of that performance, when he stepped out of his shoes, he had a heart attack and died. The audience was wildly applauding his shoes, but Bilbo never came on for his last bow.

* * *

Gene Bedini was one of the few jugglers who became a headliner. Anything he could pick up he could juggle, and sometimes he'd have as many as ten or twelve objects in the air at the same time. For the finish of his act he'd have people in the audience throw apples and oranges and pears onto the stage, and he'd catch them on the end of a fork which he held in his mouth.

At the time, Bedini was headlining the Riverside Theater, and his publicity man came up with a stunt that he thought would get a lot of publicity for Bedini. The idea was for him to go up on the roof of a ten-story building, drop a cantaloupe, and Bedini, standing on the sidewalk below, would catch it on the end of a fork in his mouth. Bedini thought the publicity guy was out of his mind. He pointed out that if he tried to catch a cantaloupe dropped from that height it would not only knock his teeth out, it would probably kill him. But the publicity man told Bedini not to worry; his idea was to take the inside out of the cantaloupe, then put the two halves back together so that it would be hollow. That way it would be light and very easy to catch. Well, Bedini went for it.

Word got around, and when the day came for the stunt there was a big crowd gathered in front of his building, including a lot of newspaper people. Bedini got into position, and just before he put the fork in his mouth he hollered up, "I'm ready. Drop it!" The publicity man dropped the hollowed-out cantaloupe, a gust of wind caught it and blew it four blocks down the street.

237

Well, that's the end of that story, and I'm not sure, but I think it was the end of that publicity man, too.

* * *

One of my very close friends is Eddie Buzzell, who was one of our top motion-picture directors. He directed many movies, including *Honolulu*, the last motion picture Gracie and I made. Eddie told me a story that I think is worth passing on. When he first came to Hollywood he went to work for Columbia Pictures. At the end of his first year he had a verbal agreement with Harry Cohn, who was the president of the company, to get a $250 weekly raise. Now, I'm not going to say that Harry Cohn was a hard man to do business with—I don't have to, everybody else has said it. When the year was up, Eddie went into Cohn's office and asked for his raise. Cohn turned on his charm. He said, "Eddie, Sam Briskin is right across the hall. He's head of production, so go in and ask him for the raise. If he okays it, it's certainly all right with me." Cohn stood up and put a fatherly hand on Eddie's shoulder. "You know me, Eddie," he continued, "when I make somebody a promise, it's a promise."

So Eddie went across the hall. When he walked into Briskin's office Sam wasn't there, but the intercom was buzzing. Eddie pushed down the lever and said, "Yeah?"

Cohn's voice came over the intercom. "Sam, Buzzell is on his way in there to ask for a raise. Don't give it to him."

Eddie pushed down the lever just as Sam walked in. Sam said, "What can I do for you, Eddie?"

Trying to act nonchalant, Eddie said, "I just left Harry Cohn's office. I'm due for a raise, and he said if it's all right with you, it's all right with him."

"Well, he's the boss," Sam said. "If it's all right with him, you've got it."

Eddie Buzzell stayed with Columbia Pictures for years and got many raises, but Harry Cohn never knew that Eddie was always $250 ahead of him.

* * *

Years ago the great actor Louis Calhern got into a cab in New York City. The driver was Jewish and spoke with an accent. He recognized Calhern and said, "Mr. Calhern, I've seen you in a lot of movies."

Calhern was flattered and said, "Thank you."

As they drove along the driver said, "What are you doing in New York?"

Calhern answered, "I'm here to appear in Shakespeare's *King Lear*."

The driver was impressed. *King Lear*, he said. "I must have seen it a dozen times. I've seen it played by all the great actors—Jacob P. Adler, Boris Tomeshevsky, David Kessler, Maurice Schwartz." Then he thought a second. He said, "Tell me something, Mr. Calhern, do you think it'll go in English?"

* * *

In the early days of small-time vaudeville all the contracts had a cancellation clause in them. If the manager didn't like your act, after the first performance you'd be canceled. At that time there was a Russian dancing act called Petrov and Sonia. Petrov was bald. And in those days the toupees they made looked awful, so Petrov used to pencil in his hair. Before every performance he used to spend about two hours sitting in front of a mirror, drawing hair on his head with a heavy black pencil. And he was a master at it. When he came onstage he looked as though he had a full head of black wavy hair. Unfortunately his hair looked better than his dancing.

He and Sonia were booked for three days into the Myrtle Theater in Brooklyn, and after the first matinee the manager canceled them. So Petrov packed his wardrobe, collected his music and his picture, rubbed out his hair, and left.

Before Rudolph Valentino became famous he worked in New York City at a place called Rector's. Rector's was a high-class restaurant, and well-to-do women used to go there in the afternoon for tea and a sandwich, and perhaps a cocktail. Well, Valentino worked there, and his job was to dance with the unescorted women. He made $18 a week and whatever he could pick up in tips from the women he danced with.

At that time one of the biggest stars on Broadway was an actress named Valeska Suratt, and one afternoon she dropped into Rector's for tea. As soon as she saw the handsome Valentino she sent a waiter over to ask him to dance with her. Well, Valentino recognized this famous actress, so in the middle of a tango he mentioned to her that he was thinking of going to Hollywood to try to make it as an actor in the movies. Miss Suratt seemed interested, so she asked him his name. He told her it was Rudolph Valentino. She stopped right in the middle of the dance, and said, "If I were you, young man, the first thing I'd do is change that name!"

So I did, and I've been calling myself George Burns ever since.

* * *

In vaudeville the opening act on a bill was usually jugglers, acrobats, roller skaters, or something like that. Well, I remember one small-time opening act called Tower and Lee. They did a comedy bicycle act. Now, as I mentioned before, in those days if the manager didn't like you, after the first matinee he would cancel you.

Tower and Lee were playing the Odeon Theater on Clinton Street, and after their first matinee the manager came back and told them they were canceled. Well, Towers had a very short temper, and when he heard this he punched the manager right in the mouth and knocked him to the floor. The manager groped around and finally found his glasses. Then, looking up at Tower, he said, "If I ever have to cancel you again, I'm gonna do it by telephone."

* * *

When I was about twenty-one or twenty-two I did an act called "Garfield and Smith—Singing, Dancing and Witty Remarks." My name was Smith. We were booked on the Pantages circuit, and headlining our unit was an act with eight beautiful girls called Sweet Sweeties. We were playing Oklahoma City, and on my way to the theater one morning I noticed a young fellow about my age sitting in a green Marmon convertible parked outside the theater—and he was crying. I couldn't figure out what he had to cry about, because a Marmon convertible in those days cost a fortune. So I started talking to him, and I found out the reason he was crying was because the girl he was in love with was having lunch in the restaurant across the street with another fellow. His named turned out to be Harold Spencer, Jr. He seemed like a nice guy, and I felt sorry for him. So I cooked up a little scheme that worked. I got one of the girls from Sweet Sweeties to have lunch with him in that same restaurant. Well, when his girlfriend saw him come in with a beautiful showgirl, she dumped the other guy and made up with Harold fast.

During that week in Oklahoma City, Harold and I became good friends, and he introduced me to a very beautiful Indian girl named Sally Trueblood. She was staying at the same hotel I was, and one night after the show she invited me down to her room to listen to some records on her Gramophone. Well, Sally was a real beauty, so I went all out and bought a bottle of scotch for two and a half dollars. And I wore my pongee robe, which I'd picked up in Vancouver a couple of weeks before. It was a beige Japanese robe

241

with very long, flowing sleeves and a red sash tied around the waist. On the back was embroidered a gold dragon with a big red tongue. I lived on the seventh floor and Sally lived on the fourth, and wearing that outfit I didn't dare take the elevator. So I walked down, holding my hands up over my head so I wouldn't step on my sleeves.

When I reached Sally's room I fixed a couple of drinks, and Sally put a record on the Gramophone. Her favorite was John McCormack singing "When Irish Eyes Are Smiling," and since it was twelve o'clock at night she stuck a towel into the Gramophone horn to muffle the sound. We no sooner got settled down when the door burst open and in came the house detective. Now, I want you to picture this: There we were; a full-blooded Indian girl and a twenty-one-year-old Jew wearing a kimono, drinking scotch, and listening to John McCormack sing "When Irish Eyes Are Smiling."

The house detective started giving me a hard time and wound up saying that he'd be willing to forget the whole thing if I'd give him $50. Well, all I had was $7, so I asked him to let me go up and talk to my partner, Garfield, to see if I could raise the rest of the money. He let me go but he made me leave my kimono as security.

Garfield only had about $7 himself, so that left me $35 short. Then I remembered that Harold Spencer lived upstairs in the penthouse. He was my last hope, so I went up to see him and told him my story. Harold's father was there, and after he heard what had happened he said, "Come on, let's go downstairs. I think I can handle this for you."

We walked into Sally's room and Harold's father fired the house detective. Harold Spencer, Sr., owned the hotel.

* * *

Novelty acts were very popular in vaudeville, and there was one act that was really a novelty. This fellow worked

242

with a chicken, and the chicken danced on one leg! The act was called Jackie Davis and Chick Fowler. The fellow's name was Chick Fowler.

Chick was a good entertainer, but he liked to drink a lot. Every once in a while he'd pour a little booze in a saucer for the chicken, and the chicken got to like it. He not only got to like it, he got to love it. Half of the time he was smashed. Well, it was tough enough for the chicken to dance on one leg when he was sober, but when he was smashed it was murder. Before you knew it, it got so they couldn't get a job.

I ran into Chick one day and said, "Chick, how are things going?"

He said, "Not good, George, things are so tough that last night I pretty near ate my partner."

I said, "Chick, you wouldn't do a thing like that!"

He shook his head and said, "Of course not. But I must admit I ate the leg he wasn't using!"

Another true story.

* * *

During the time I was doing the Burns and Allen show on radio most of the variety shows were using big bands. Our band leader was Artie Shaw. When we moved the show from New York to California, Artie had a problem with James Petrillo, who was then head of the musicians' union. One of the key men in Artie's band was his trumpet player, and naturally Artie wanted to bring him along to California. But Petrillo wouldn't allow it. Artie was very upset because this trumpet player was extremely important to him, but Petrillo wouldn't give in.

The day after we arrived in California I was on my way to the Brown Derby restaurant to have a drink, and there on the newsstand was a headline that read, LANA TURNER DIVORCES ARTIE SHAW. There was a picture of Lana in a sweater, and she looked absolutely beautiful. Inside the Derby, there was Artie at the bar having a drink. I knew how bad he must have felt about losing a beautiful girl like Lana, so I put my arm around him and said, "Artie, don't take it too hard. Things like that happen to everybody."

Artie looked at me and said, "To hell with Petrillo—I'll find myself a trumpet player out here!"

* * *

One of our really big stars in the twenties was a lady named Blossom Seeley. She was not only an exciting personality onstage, but she created many innovations that were later used by other artists. Blossom was the first to snap her fingers when she sang. She was the first to put one foot over the footlights so she'd be closer to the audience. She was the first to use a baby spotlight over her head to give the effect of a halo. When she played nightclubs she was the first to use a small upright piano, which she wheeled from table to table. And she was the first performer to get down on one knee to sing a song.

Blossom was born in California, and at seventeen she was playing nightclubs in San Francisco on the Barbary Coast. She was known as Baby Blossom, and at seventeen she was the most voluptuous and sexy thing you've ever seen. In her act she'd come out wearing a skin-tight black leotard, and around her waist was strapped a tiger's head which hung in front of her. While she was singing, to show their appreciation the men would toss silver dollars at her. Blossom had a string attached to the tiger's head, and when the men tossed the silver dollars she'd pull the string and catch the money in the tiger's mouth. (Another first!) No matter where the men threw those silver dollars her little tiger's head was there to catch them. I once said to Blossom, "Did you ever miss catching one of those silver dollars?"

"Are you kidding" she said, "I not only never missed, I got so good at it I could even throw back change!"

It wasn't long before Blossom became famous, and she and Al Jolson were starring in a show at the Winter Garden

244

theater in New York. One of her big numbers was a song called "Toddling the Toddle-O." She was a sensation and took encore after encore. When she sang the last chorus she got down on one knee, and the audience went wild.

Well, Al Jolson watched this from the wings—and that man was no dummy. He came out onstage and got down on one knee with her. But Blossom made one mistake—she got up—but Jolson never did.

Later in her career Blossom married a talented young singer named Benny Fields. They worked together and became one of the great teams in vaudeville. Their closing number was a song called "In a Little Spanish Town," and Benny would stand behind Blossom, put his arms around her waist, and play his guitar in front of her. For an exit, as they were singing they would do a little side-shuffle step into the wings.

If it was a good audience, Blossom would snuggle back against Benny as they shuffled off. As I said, this little lady knew how to snuggle. The audience loved it, but not nearly as much as Benny.

That was, if it was a good audience. If it was a bad audience, Blossom always blamed it on Benny. There was no snuggling, and as they shuffled off she would stomp on Benny's toes with her high-spiked heels. Whenever I saw Benny limping to his dressing room I knew there was a bad audience out front.

* * *

When I lived on the Lower East Side there was a fellow in our neighborhood named Harry Farley, whose greatest ambition in life was to be on the police force. He tried and tried, but he couldn't make it. In those days you had to be at least 5'9" to be a New York City policeman, and Harry was only 5'8". Well, Harry was so desperate to make the police force that he rigged up a stretching machine in his basement and stretched himself every day for four months.

245

If Harry had lived, he would have been one of New York's finest!

* * *

Just for a change of mood I thought I'd throw in this next story for you readers who like tragedy. If you don't like tragedy, read the policeman story again.

There used to be a small-time dancing act called The Goldie Boys; two brothers named Jack and Phil Goldie. It was not the greatest act in the world, and they were getting nowhere. So Jack's wife, Nettie, talked him into giving up the act and opening a delicatessen. Jack had a friend, an East Side gangster known as Crazy Manny, and Manny agreed to lend Jack $2,000 to open the store. However, Jack had to promise to pay it back in three months.

Well, the delicatessen turned out to be just as bad as the Goldie Boys. At the end of three months Jack didn't have the money, so he went to Crazy Manny and asked for more time. But Crazy Manny wouldn't go for it. "Nothing doing," he said. "A deal is a deal. This is Friday—if you don't have the money by Monday morning at nine o'clock, I'll kill you!"

Jack tried everything possible, but he just couldn't come up with the money. So, after a sleepless night, at nine o'clock on Monday morning there was a knock on Jack's door. He knew this was it. There was nothing else he could do, so he took a gun and killed himself. What he didn't know was that the knock on the door was his brother Phil coming to tell him that Crazy Manny had been shot and killed the night before.

Isn't that a darling tragedy?

* * *

One of the vaudeville acts I did which I forgot to mention in the book was called "Ruby Delmar and Friend." I was

Friend. It wasn't great billing, but by that time I did so many acts I ran out of names. Ruby was a beautiful girl except that she was bowlegged. She always looked as though someone had stolen her cello. From her waist up, she was stunning. From her waist down, I was prettier.

In those days all the girls wore short skirts. But Ruby was self-conscious about her legs, so she always wore long skirts. Even on the stage her dress was right down to the floor. She was a great whirlwind dancer, but nobody knew it because everything she did was hidden by that skirt. When I was on the stage with her I'd look out at the audience, and they looked so confused—they knew something was going on under that skirt, but they didn't know what. So I had to explain to the audience that she was dancing. Once I had to explain it to the police.

Anyway, our agent said he couldn't get us any more work with Ruby wearing those long dresses. So I figured out the answer. I had Ruby wear a short skirt, changed the act to Latin music, and got Ruby a bongo drum. She was a sensation. She was the only girl who could do a whirlwind tango and still have room for the bongo. She was such a big hit that she teamed up with a bowlegged fellow and got rid of me. I really couldn't blame her; I had no place to hold my bongo.

There's a finish to this story. Ruby married her partner and I went to the wedding. It was a beautiful affair except for one thing—they had to walk down both aisles.

* * *

Years ago when Gracie and I were doing radio we hired Tony Martin as our singer. At that time Tony was very young and had been working as a saxophone player with a small band in Oakland. He sang with a saxophone around his neck, and he'd always play with the buttons on the sax while he was singing because he didn't know what to do with his hands.

When he came on our show he was just a singer and didn't need the saxophone. On his first show he sang "Begin the Beguine," and he was so used to playing with his buttons that when he got to the second chorus he lost his pants.

* * *

Several years ago I came up with an idea for a publicity stunt that I thought was tremendous. I was sure it would break into newpapers all over the country. Everybody always kids me about my singing, so I decided to take advantage of it and insure my voice for a million dollars. A brilliant idea, wasn't it?

I was so excited I couldn't wait to rush down to the insurance company, and I took a cassette and a tape recorder with me so the insurance man could hear my voice. I explained to him that I wanted to insure my voice for a million dollars and I played my cassette for him. It was one of my best numbers: a syncopated version of "Yankee Doodle Blues" with a yodeling finish. He sat there and listened patiently to the whole thing, then he just looked at me and said, "Mr. Burns, you should have come to us before you had the accident."

This kid made me kind of nervous. That was a very funny line and I couldn't think of a way to top it. But it didn't dull my enthusiasm any; I kept right on punching. I said, "Look, this is my natural way of singing, and you don't have to worry about having to pay any claims. Whatever is going to happen to my voice has already happened."

He sighed and said, "Mr. Burns, we're talking about a million-dollar policy. I could understand if you sang like Robert Goulet, or John Raitt, or Alfred Drake. They have trained voices."

I said, "Okay, so mine isn't even housebroken. But let me tell you the truth. This whole idea is a publicity stunt. I take out this big policy, it breaks in all the papers, I pay the first premium, and then we cancel."

He shook his head and said, "Mr. Burns, you're wasting your time. If my boss heard that cassette with that yodeling finish, there's no way in the world he'd approve the policy."

I said, "Do me a favor. Take the cassette inside, play it for your boss, and tell the truth. Tell him it's just a publicity stunt."

He smiled and said, "Mr. Burns, I know my boss, and it just won't work."

"I'll make a deal with you," I said. "If your boss doesn't okay that policy, I'll buy you a new suit of clothes."

He shrugged and took the cassette into the next office. Five minutes later he came out and said, "Mr. Burns, make that a blue suit with double vents in the jacket and dark-blue piping on the lapels."

Well, I never got the policy, but to show you what a sweet man I am, I threw in a monogrammed handkerchief for his breast pocket.

* * *

There was a very funny and zany act in vaudeville called Duffy and Sweeney. This particular time they were booked for a week into the Orpheum Theater in New Orleans. When they arrived they checked into the Roosevelt Hotel. Now, in those days you could get a double room for $3 a day, and that's what Duffy and Sweeney wanted. Somehow the hotel clerk got mixed up and instead of a double room gave them a whole suite. When they got upstairs and saw this elegant suite, Duffy picked up the phone and called down to the desk. He said, "How much is this suite?" And the clerk answered, "Twenty dollars a day."

"Well," Duffy said, "if we're going to pay twenty dollars a day, you better send up another Gideon Bible."

* * *

In reading over the galleys of this book I notice I didn't mention my friend Jack Haley. Jack and I have been very close friends all of our lives, and if I don't mention his name, he may never talk to me again. So I better mention it. Here it is: Jack Haley!

* * *

In case you're wondering, let me tell you how this book got its subtitle, "They Still Love Me in Altoona!" When I was about eighteen I did a single and was using the name of Willie Saks. My billing was "Willie Saks and His Little Derby Hat." I don't say this was the worst act in show business, but if they'd taken a poll, I would have been right up there. Actually, I was what you called a disappointment act. I'd sit by the telephone with my grip packed, and in case an actor got sick or broke his leg, I was ready to jump in and take his place.

Well, after sitting in my room for about six weeks my phone rang, and it was a booking agent. An actor who was booked into Altoona had gotten sick and they needed somebody in a hurry. So off I went. I got there just in time to make the first matinee. My opening song went like this:

> You'll notice on the program where it mentions all the acts,
> If you take a look at Number 2, you'll see the name of Saks;
> It doesn't say company or anything like that,
> It simply says assisted by his little derby hat—
> Ohhhhhhhh,
> There is a little mystery what this little hat can do,
> It has a little history that I must tell to you;
> It doesn't sing, it doesn't dance or anything like that,
> It simply says assisted by his little derby hat—
> Ohhhhhhhh . . .

I sang about four more verses, then I told a few jokes, sang another song, and finished with an imitation of Pat Rooney. Don't ask me why, but I was a big hit. I took about six bows. It scared me. I was so used to being a flop I figured I must be doing something wrong. After the matinee the manager came into my dressing room, and he was so happy about the way I had gone over that he asked me to stay and finish out the week. I was bowled over; I'd never played a full week anywhere before. Well, I finished the week, and after each show it was the same thing—I was a smash.

Three weeks later I was back waiting in my room again, and the phone rang. An actor had sprained an ankle and I was booked into Mechanicsville. I couldn't wait to get there; this time I was full of confidence. I swaggered out on the stage, did my act, and the people despised me.

And that's the way it went until I was twenty-seven. But whenever I got to feeling low, I could always look back and say to myself, *"They Still Love Me in Altoona"*!

Benny and Burns. *Photo by Trans Ocean Press.*

251